THE NEXT

Move

OF

God

FUCHSIA PICKETT

CREATION HOUSE

BOOKS ABOUT SPIRIT-LED LIVING

ORLANDO, FLORIDA

Creation House
Strang Communications Company
600 Rinehart Road
Lake Mary, FL 32746
Phone: (407) 333-3132
Fax: (407) 333-7100

Unless otherwise noted, all Scripture quotations are from the
King James Version of the Bible.

Scripture quotations marked NAS are from the New American Standard Bible. Copyright © 1960, 1962, 1963, 1968,
1971, 1972, 1973, 1975, 1977 by the Lockman
Foundation. Used by permission.

First printing, November 1994
Second printing, March 1995

Dedicated to all the faithful saints
throughout the body of Christ who
have been so supportive to me and my ministry.
I am grateful for their receptivity to the Word
and for their prayers for health, safety, strength
and fresh anointing as I travel so extensively.

Contents

Part 3
The Charismatic Renewal and the Next Move of God

Part 4
The New Blessing of the Next Move of God

Part One

Personal Revelation
of the Next Move of God

One

THE PROCLAMATION

Revival Is Coming

Wilt thou not revive us again: that thy people may rejoice in thee? (Ps. 85:6).

For more than thirty years I have proclaimed, shouted and declared, without wavering, that the Church is going to experience a great revival before the return of Jesus. I have seen in the Scriptures the promise of the Holy Spirit moving in the earth to bring a wonderful revival to His Church and, subsequently, a great harvest of souls. The Lord also gave me a vision in 1963 of some of the things He is going to do in the church world in these last days in which we are living.

I believed the proclamation of a great revival and harvest of souls when I began to preach it. I believe it now more than ever because of the evidences of revival I see. What joy it gives me to see what the Holy Spirit revealed to me in vision form coming to pass more than thirty years later.

A Vision of Revival

In 1959 I was healed of a genetic bone disease that had taken the lives of several members of my family and was believed to be unto death for me as well.[1] That same day I was baptized in the Holy Spirit. Until then my theology had not accepted either healing or the baptism in the Holy Spirit as biblical. Through these wonderful experiences, God "invaded" my life, sending His Holy Spirit to take up residence inside me as my divine teacher. He began to reveal His Word to me as I had never known it, though I had been a professor and minister of the Methodist church for seventeen years.

Four years later, while I was ministering in a church in Klamath Falls, Oregon, God took me "into the Spirit" for two days. The Lord told me that if I would remain in the sanctuary and wait upon Him, He would show me things to come in His Church and in the world when He poured out the fullness of His Spirit. As I waited there in prayer He took me into the heavenlies and let me see the revival that is coming. As He wrote it on the screen of my mind and spirit, I saw it more clearly than I see the faces of people.

Hydroelectric Power Plant

The Holy Spirit used the analogy of a hydroelectric power plant to explain to me what He was going to do. (I knew nothing about electricity; I couldn't have fixed a light switch if my life depended upon it.) Hour after hour He carried me into the revelation of this vision, showing me heaven's *dunamis* power.

The Greek word for the power of the Holy Spirit is *dunamis*, from which we derive our word *dynamo*. The analogy of a hydroelectric power plant was a dramatic word picture to reveal the *dunamis* work of the Holy Spirit.[2] It should not have surprised me that the Holy Spirit would describe His working in the heavenlies using such an analogy.

Above the Church, high in the heavenlies, I saw the excavation for the building of a huge hydroelectric power plant. God laid the solid concrete foundation carefully, measuring the sand that went into it exactly. He cleansed everything and placed every screen and tubule in order precisely as it should be. Then He erected the power plant section by section. I saw the pipes; the dam and all its massive gates; out from which He ran prime lines, primary lines and secondary lines through great transformers to many points of distribution. After that, He began to fill the reservoirs with water, teaching me that unless a certain level of water was maintained the high-powered dynamo could not function properly.

As I watched, I saw a church without walls. An awesome divine power was flowing down through the pulpits, out to the people and then through them to the world. Above this power plant I saw Christ, the Head of the Church, holding that gigantic power plant in His hands. At the same time, however, it seemed as though He were the One being poured through that power plant, down into the church and out to the world — a great harvest field, golden and ripe unto harvest.

Networking Churches

Somehow I understood that He was flowing His living water only to churches where deep wells and reservoirs had been dug. In the vision, I saw pipes being placed underground from one fountainhead to another — from church to church. The pipes formed a network of churches, connecting those with deep wells that He had dug and filled with His living water — the living Word.

I wished it was going to all churches, but I realized that many churches could not tap into this living water because they had no reservoir. And I heard the words, "Deep calleth unto deep at the noise of thy waterspouts" (Ps. 42:7).

In 1963 there was little evidence of such networking of churches and ministers. Nevertheless, I understood that He was showing me a network of churches that had been dug out through which He would flow His great flood of truth. The "digging" would happen as pastors and believers obeyed God and allowed the dealings of God to work in their lives. By their yielded obedience to the Holy Spirit and His Word they would become reservoirs of truth. From these churches His power would flow throughout all the world.

Although no specific cities were named, I saw five geographical areas within the United States that would become vital centers for this divine power. When a vast network of churches had been filled with living water, God would pull a great switch and open *all* the gates of truth that have been dammed up by man. I saw the release of stream after stream of truth that God wanted to flow freely in the Church, but that truth had been dammed up behind denominational walls erected by man.

Then, as the vision continued to unfold to me, in my spirit I heard the water — His Word — begin to run. Churches that had their reservoirs prepared began to fill up with water. They were ready for God to pull the switch and open the gates of truth from that great dynamo. I remembered Jesus' promise to those who believed on Him. He said: "Out of his belly shall flow rivers of living water" (John 7:38b). This verse speaks figuratively of "the effects of the operation of the Holy Spirit in and through the believer."[3]

When God releases His *dunamis* power in this next move of God, rivers of living water will flow out of our innermost beings. Habakkuk's prophecy will become a reality: "For the earth shall be filled with the knowledge of the glory of the Lord, as the waters cover the sea" (Hab. 2:14). When those gates of truth are finally opened we are going to see an "old-fashioned, heaven-sent, sky-blue, sin-killing, gully-washing revival."

Scientific Documentation

I transcribed my vision of the hydroelectric plant onto paper. Leon McGuire, in whose home I was staying, took the transcript to the Pacific Power Company in Oregon and asked to see the head engineer. He told him he would like to leave a transcript for him to critique, saying, "It is very important to us that we understand this material and know whether or not it is correct. The person who wrote it is deeply concerned as to its accuracy. If you would not mind taking some time to critique it, we would greatly appreciate it." The engineer agreed to do so.

When my host returned to the power company a few days

later, the president of the company wanted to see him. A receptionist ushered him into the office of the president. After greeting him kindly, the president asked, "Where did you get this information?"

My host responded, "What would you say if I told you that a little woman who cannot fix a light switch wrote it?"

"I would say she is pulling your leg," the president retorted. "This paper is one of the most scientific I have ever read. There are words and terms in here that only a few master electricians know and understand. Some of these terms are even used by men in the Pentagon. Whoever wrote this paper was a master electrician."

"Please forgive me," my host responded, "I should not have said it was a little lady who wrote it; she just copied it down. The Master Electrician — the Holy Spirit — described it to her."

Construction in Progress

At the time of my vision, my Father said to me, "I am running the pipes now. And this time when I pull that great power switch and release all the rivers of my living Word in their fullness, no demon, devil, man or denomination will ever dam it up again. I will do a quick work; I am going to bring the revival that will result in the ingathering of the great harvest of souls."

1. God also let me see what the ministry of the local church will be when His Spirit is poured out.

2. The local churches would use the power of the living Word to take care of the needs of the people who gravitated to them.

3. In this way, the vision for the ministry of each local church would develop according to the needs that presented themselves.

4. Whatever type of people — youth, elderly, poor — that gravitated to a local church would receive full pastoral care.

5. I understood that the believers in these churches would also go outside their four walls to take care of the wounded, hurt, lame, rejected and poor. They would feed the hungry and train disciples. They would teach ministers, raising them up to take the church into her inheritance.

I also saw the printed page rolling, producing Christian literature. I watched the Church march into the heavenlies in the Spirit and invade the evil powers of the media. I saw the grainfields of the world ready to be harvested, and my Father said it was going to happen soon.

I heard the sound of waters rolling in my ears from October to December of that year. Finally I prayed, "Father, if it please You, take this sound away from my ears and turn it inside. But let me continue to hear the river of Your living Word."

Since that vision was given thirty years ago I have been to many churches in America where I heard the sound of those waters, confirming that they are reservoirs that are now being connected to the network of pipes. In churches on the isles of Trinidad, the Bahamas and Hawaii, and in nations in South America I have heard those supernatural waters running. I'm sure they are running in places I have not been as well. God's truth is being stored up, the water levels are rising, and God is getting ready to release His power in the earth in Holy Ghost revival.

Escapist Mentality

People raised their eyebrows in disbelief when I first began to preach what I had seen in that vision. Thirty years ago the Church was not focused on revival. Much of the Church was caught in the passive, faithless attitude of "hanging on a little while longer." Her theology did not accept the fact of a great harvest of souls. Many were simply waiting to be raptured. Even her hymns reflected her pessimistic philosophy. A line of a favorite hymn sung in those years says: "I'm going through whatever others do...I'll make my way with the Lord's despised few."

Many Christians believed Jesus would steal them away from this world one night as from a fire escape. Then, they believed, the world would be sorry they didn't know who the Church was. They thought the media would send reporters throughout the world to discover the facts about the disappearance of the Church. My response to that whole idea is, "Jesus does not have to steal me; I'm already His — He bought me."

Christians who were bogged down in this escapist mentality exhorted each other pitifully: "Just hang on, honey. God will get us out of here soon." For many, our infinite, omnipotent God seemed barely able to withstand the onslaught of evil, and the Church seemed weak and impotent. Such unbelief denied God's power to establish the glorious Church He has promised in His Word.

The more the Holy Spirit taught me from His Book, the more I recognized the fallacy of the Church's escapist mentality. The Church *is* going to meet Him, but before we do, the world *is* going to know we have been here! We will not have to sneak out onto a smoldering fire escape some night, dressed in smoke-filled, soot-covered tatters to be rescued from the darkness of this world system. God is returning for a glorious Church without spot or wrinkle (Eph. 5:27). The reality of a glorious Church should convince those who question that revival will be a precursor to His coming. Only revival can establish that glorious Church.

Revival or Harvest?

Later, my Teacher told me that I had my terms mixed up, that what I was calling revival was actually harvest. Revival is bringing back to life that which is dying; harvest is a reaping of souls. The reviving of the Church is necessary before there can be a harvest of souls.

Unless we understand all that is involved in revival we cannot understand what God is doing in the Church today. God has the Church in His hands and is beginning to breathe His resurrection life into her. That is revival. Revival involves repentance and a return to our first love for God. In the process of reviving His Church, God is cleansing her, circumcising her and empowering her. If we misunderstand this sometimes painful work of the Holy Spirit, we may perceive that this pruning process brings defeat and loss — not revival — especially when it results in people leaving our churches.

To the contrary, God's divine pruning process removes dead wood from the vine so the Church can bring forth good fruit, fruit that will remain, in preparation for the real harvest that is coming. The life God is giving the Church through revival is going to result in a harvest of souls that will reach throughout the world. I believe thousands of souls will be saved in a day.

The great harvest that is yet to come must wait until the Church submits to the process of revival. Those who resist the cleansing work of the Holy Spirit may fall away, causing an initial decrease of members in our churches. But after the Church has been pruned, circumcised and revived, harvest will be imminent. In that harvest the Church will realize a great ingathering of souls.

The "Third Day" Message

The message of the significance of the "third day" closely parallels the understanding of revival. Throughout the Bible, the third day represents new beginnings and resurrection life (see Gen. 22:4; 2 Kin. 20:5; Matt. 12:40; Matt. 27:63). Hosea, the prophet, declared:

"Come, and let us return unto the Lord: for he hath torn, and he will heal us; he hath smitten, and he will bind us up. After two days will he revive us: in the third day he will raise us up, and we shall live in his sight. Then shall we know, if we follow on to know the Lord: his going forth is prepared as the morning; and he shall come unto us as the rain, as the latter and former rain unto the earth" (Hosea 6:1-3).

I knew God had commanded Joshua to cross the Jordan and to possess the promised land on the third day (Josh. 1:11). I declared that this new move of God would bring the Church into a land that we had never possessed, just as Israel entered the promised land under Joshua's leadership. Joshua is a biblical type of Jesus, our heavenly Joshua, who is going to take His Church into the promised land.

What is the promised land? Some have taught that it is heaven. But it cannot be heaven. There are no giants in heaven and no battles to be won as there were in the promised land. Although many of our gospel songs refer to Canaan as heaven, it is a fact that we are going to enter Canaan before we go to heaven.

In my book, *God's Dream*, I shared the understanding my Father gave me of how the Church would enter into her inheritance — the promised land — as it was revealed to the apostle Paul. Paul received a revelation of the fulfillment of God's dream for a *family* conformed to His image, recipients of His character, having the *family* spirit of love. He saw the Church filled with transformed people fulfilling God's eternal plan. Paul understood God's eternal purpose to build a glorious Church, and he stated:

> Till we all come in the unity of the faith, and of the knowledge of the Son of God, unto a perfect man, unto the measure of the stature of the fullness of Christ (Eph. 4:13).

Israel, a type of the Church, gives us a pattern of what the Church must experience to enter the promised land. In order to enter their inheritance, Israel had to defeat the Hittites, Amorites, Canaanites, Perizzites, Hivites and the Jebusites.

For the Church to enter into its inheritance, she must defeat the "ites" of the works of the flesh Paul listed for the Galatians (Gal. 5:19-21). She must come into the maturity Paul described throughout his epistles. He taught that the Church should be filled with righteousness, peace and joy in the Holy Ghost, and learn to walk in humility, holiness and unity.

We will know we have entered the promised land when

Jesus' high priestly prayer in the seventeenth chapter of John becomes a reality in the Church:

> That they all may be one; as thou, Father, art in me, and I in thee, that they also may be one in us: that the world may believe that thou hast sent me (John 17:21).

This can only be realized through a mighty work of the Holy Spirit yet to come. I believe the purpose of God is to bring His Church into the promised land on the third day.

Understanding, then, that the promised land is a place of maturity in our walk with God as individuals and as the Church, some may still be wondering, "What is the third day?" While our purpose here is not to fully explore the significance of the third day as taught in the Scriptures, it is a fact that God chose to intervene in mankind's affairs in special ways on the third day. It is an interesting study to trace through the Bible the promises of the third day.

Although God dwells in eternity, He deals with mankind in time. But His perspective of time is necessarily different from ours. The apostle Peter wrote that "one day is with the Lord as a thousand years, and a thousand years as one day" (2 Pet. 3:8). As we consider that fact, when our calendar turns to 2000 A.D., we will have completed two "days," and will be entering a "third day" era in God's perspective. Because of the biblical pattern of God's intervention into the affairs of men on the "third day," many believe that God is going to do something special in and through His Church in the next century.

Evidences of Revival

Indeed, for the last few years as I have traveled throughout our nation and others, I have seen evidences of revival breaking upon the Church. I have heard ministers using these phrases: "the new wave," "the new revival," "the latter rain" and "the Joshua generation." These phrases are all synonymous — each a word picture expressing the next move of God.

I heard marvelous reports of revival and manifestations of the harvest in many third world nations. As I traveled to some of these countries, I saw Holy Ghost revival happening before my eyes. The churches were alive to God; thousands of men and women, youth and children were swept into the kingdom and miracles became the norm rather than the exception.

I got excited! I knew the *dunamis* power of God was bringing new life to these third world churches that would result in a harvest of souls. Yet I realized that although revival also belonged to us in the Western world, events taking place in the American church seemed to contradict the fact that God was ready to pour out His Spirit in a new way in our nation. Many American churches were experiencing losses and painful situations.

I cried out, "Father, where is the Church? Why hasn't the American church plugged into your *dunamis* power?"

In His faithfulness, He answered me and helped me to see what was happening in many churches. As my eyes opened to His perspective, I was not devastated by what seemed to be contrary reports to what God had promised. God's Word always gives hope in the midst of the most difficult circumstances. In the chapters that follow, I want to share God's eternal plan for the Church. That plan unfolds as we identify the present dwelling place for much of the Church — crouched in the safety of a cave!

Two

WHERE IS THE CHURCH?

Cave Dwellers Anonymous

"To revive the spirit of the humble, and to revive the heart of the contrite ones" (Is. 57:15).

I travel extensively throughout our nation, teaching in hundreds of churches and at many conferences, and at one time I was shocked and grieved in my spirit by what I had seen happening in the body of Christ. All appearances seemed contrary to what God promised and to what was happening in the nations of the third world.

I also served (and still serve) as one of twenty-nine persons from twenty-five countries who are trustees of the International Third World Revival Fellowship. The wonderful reports of how God was moving among the third world nations were a sad contrast to the reports of conflict and moral decay in the Church in our nation.

The media had begun to defame and slander the Church in America — and not without cause. Leaders who had fallen to immorality or misappropriation of funds received daily publicity, and the Church became the laughingstock of relentless and merciless media attacks. There was a great falling away of Christians, and many churches suffered division from within.

Many confused and bewildered ministers came to me for counseling because of the turmoil in their churches. These men and women had received revelations of great truths from the Scriptures by the Holy Spirit, filling them with great anticipation for a coming revival. Yet, instead of the move of God they were expecting to see, they were experiencing opposition from the enemy in their churches.

The Cry of the Prophet

The lament of the prophet filled our own hearts, and we cried with him: "Revive thy work in the midst of the years" (Hab. 3:2).

We longed for the promise to be fulfilled that God gave to Isaiah: "I dwell on a high and holy place, and also with the contrite and lowly of spirit in order to revive the spirit of the lowly and to revive the heart of the contrite" (Is. 57:15, NAS). Two prerequisites for revival which are revealed in this verse are *lowliness* or *humility,* and a *contrite spirit.* Perhaps, I mused, we did not qualify.

I began to wonder, Where is the revival? Where is the next move of God so many have believed was on the horizon? "Why are so many leaders falling," I cried out to my Father, "while others are hurting from wounds inflicted by Christian brothers and sisters? *Where is the Church?* What is happening to her?"

The "Hidden" Church

When I refer to the Church in this way, I am not speaking of an institution, organization or denomination. I am referring to the biblical concept of a living organism — the body of Christ. This body is made of true believers who seek God sincerely and desire to do His will. Wherever there are people who are surrendered to the Lordship of Jesus, who love and serve Him, God is there to reveal Himself and to build His Church.

The answer my Father gave me flooded my heart with understanding and renewed hope. He told me that He had hidden the Church away from the eyes of the world today much as He hid David in the cave of Adullam in Saul's day (1 Sam. 22:1).

God had taken the Church — the living organism of which Christ is the Head — and placed her in a "cave." He was preparing His Church, in much the same way that God had prepared David, to reign in the kingdom. In spite of the unpleasant implications of "cave dwelling," my Father's answer brought hope to my heart.

King David's Preparation

During the time of his reign, Saul had a lot going for him. He was a mighty warrior who had been anointed by God and was loved by his people. But he was also impetuous at times and was given to angry fits and jealousies. God allowed a series of trials to test Saul's principles, but Saul failed one test after another.

At Gilgal Saul refused to wait for direction from God and assumed he could choose his own direction (1 Sam. 13:8-9).

Soon after this failed test, his greed led him to ignore God's instructions to destroy the Amalekites and their herds, and he kept the best animals for himself, lying to the prophet Samuel about what he had done (1 Sam. 15:3). He fell so far from his pursuit of godliness that ultimately he consulted a witch for advice, having lost the presence of God.

When one is proven unfit for God's service, sooner or later that person is removed from his or her position of authority. King Saul was definitely on his way out. The way David handled this transition of power is worth noting.

David received three separate anointings of God for leadership. As a young lad, years before his cave experience, the great prophet Samuel had anointed David to be king over Israel in Saul's place (1 Sam. 16:11-13).

I wonder who believed this anointing was valid — David? Samuel? his brothers? his father? Perhaps they were the few who did. Knowledge of that anointing did not go much farther, for fear of the king's response.

His young life gave evidence that he had been anointed of God. It was after this first anointing that David killed Goliath and found himself enlisted in the service of King Saul. During those years he became a beloved minstrel, his anointing able to dispel the evil spirit that tormented Saul (1 Sam. 16:23). Then he became a great warrior against the Philistines, enjoying such success that he gained recognition throughout the land. The women's songs, as they proclaimed that Saul had slain his thousands, but David his tens of thousands, energized Saul's jealousy against him (1 Sam. 18:7-8). During this time, the Bible declares that "David behaved himself wisely in all his ways; and the Lord was with him"(1 Sam 18:14).

Saul became so jealous of David that he pursued him to

kill him, but David escaped and found himself hiding in a cave (1 Sam. 22:1). Four hundred men who were experiencing distress, debt and discontent defected from King Saul and joined David's army (1 Sam. 22:2). During those years of cave life David trained these desperate men, forging a loyalty of heart and strength of character in them through the many battles they fought together. Later, when David was crowned king, these once desperate men became David's faithful leaders.

On two occasions when Saul was in David's hand, David refused to take his life. He would not touch God's anointed. He had conquered one of the greatest temptations of the human heart — to judge God's anointed. We can observe the godly character that was being formed in David through his responses to these situations.

The demise of Saul continued until his tragic, violent death on the battlefield. David, the pursued, mourned his leader's death, crying: "How are the mighty fallen" (2 Sam. 1:27).

After Saul's death, the men of Judah came to him and anointed him for a second time (2 Sam. 2:1-4). For seven years he reigned over the tribe of Judah while Ishbosheth, Saul's son, reigned over the remaining tribes of Israel. After Ishbosheth was killed in battle, the tribes of Israel came to David and anointed him as king over all of Israel and Judah, thus fulfilling the prophet's word given many years earlier.

Despite David's anointing as a youth, and his military feats of heroism, God required him to experience the discipline of the cave before going to the throne.

Perhaps it was the honorable way David handled the persecutions of Saul that won the hearts of the men he would one day lead. Or it may have been the victorious, godly character he developed through his cave experiences that prepared him to receive the second and third anointings. Thus his life would follow the pattern of God's dealings with other spiritual leaders such as Joseph, Moses and even Jesus, who conquered temptation from Satan himself in the wilderness before He began His ministry.

The Church has been experiencing the discomfort and trials of the rigors of "cave life" — those circumstances and situations that require our obedience and bring a humbling to our hearts. When we respond correctly, these cave disciplines forge the character of God in our hearts thus preparing us for sonship, leadership, throneship and "brideship."

My Father said to me, "My daughter, I am doing a work in the Church that the world does not understand. The difficult situations the Church is enduring are training and preparing her for the throne. When the Church is ready to come out of the cave, she is going to be different. The world will see Jesus in the Church, of which He is the Head."

The Work of Circumcision

There is a beautiful parallel to the work of the cave in another Old Testament example. Historically, after the death of Moses, God told Joshua to "command the people, saying...within three days you shall pass over this Jordan, to go in to possess the land" (Josh. 1:11). Thus he led them into the promised land on the third day. Joshua is a type of Jesus — as our heavenly Joshua, Jesus will lead His Church into the promised land.

But there is more revelation in this parallel of Joshua marching the children of Israel into the promised land on the third day than we may have understood. As I taught the third day message, the Lord told me that I had left out part of the story. As I read the biblical account again, He said to me: "I told Joshua that before he could take the new generation into the land they had to be circumcised."

In a literal sense, circumcision is an operation performed by a rabbi or skilled physician for the sake of procreation as well as for hygienic purposes. It removes excess flesh that could hinder reproduction. This painful cutting away of flesh represents a covenant of obedience established between God and His people.

In the New Testament, Paul refers to the circumcision of the heart (Rom. 2:29). He explained to the Colossians that we are circumcised "with the circumcision made without hands, in putting off the body of the sins of the flesh by the circumcision of Christ" (Col. 2:11).

With anticipation, we have proclaimed that the Joshua generation is marching into the land to conquer our enemies. But in our excitement, many have not understood that circumcision is necessary before we can enjoy the victory of the promised land.

No one considers surgery to be a pleasant experience. But we submit to it because it results in the removal of that which hinders health and life. The Scriptures teach that "the Word of God is quick, and powerful, and sharper than any two-edged sword, piercing even to the dividing asunder of soul and spirit, and of the joints and marrow, and is a discerner of the thoughts and intents of the heart" (Heb. 4:12). We cannot receive the Word of God without experiencing the pain of its "dividing" work in our souls. God requires the Church to pass through the painful place of circumcision in order to enter into her inheritance.

God is removing the "flesh programs" in our lives and churches, and tearing down man's kingdoms in order for the new generation to be what God wants it to be. He is cleansing the Church; changing her motivation, attitudes, priorities and character; and training her to be His army. The enemy's knife cuts for destruction, but the Holy Spirit's knife brings ultimate healing. I believe the Church will soon recover from this painful process of circumcision.

Understanding the Types

From these two biblical types — David's preparation in the cave, and the process of circumcision — the Holy Spirit showed me the present position of the Church in the purposes of God. God's purpose is to cleanse and establish the Church in His divine plan — not to destroy it. Today, as in the days of Isaiah the prophet, God's desire is "to revive the spirit of the humble, and to revive the heart of the contrite ones" (Is. 57:15). As we meet the requirements of humility and contrition of heart, we will be qualified for sonship, leadership, throneship and "brideship." Our God will dwell with us, and revival will become a reality.

The End of Training

Although David thought he was fleeing for his life from the pursuit of Saul, his plight was part of God's purpose for his development as a leader. His cave experience prepared him for the leadership the throne would require. The men who followed David also benefitted from the cave experiences, developing godly character as well.

29

So it is with the Church. In order for the Church to become "more than conquerors" (Rom. 8:37), and fulfill God's eternal plan, godly character has to be formed in her through divinely ordained "cave" experiences. The Church can expect the same kind of triumph David experienced.

David's Mighty Men

The men who had come to David in distress, debt and discontent became "mighty men of valor" (1 Chron. 12:21). They were armed with bows and were able to shoot arrows right- or left-handed (1 Chron. 12:2). This signifies that they were balanced to face any enemy threat, diversified in their skills and dangerous because of their abilities. The Scriptures admonish believers to "fight the good fight of faith" (1 Tim. 6:12). The cave develops soldiers into great fighters!

The Scriptures tell us also that these brave, battle-ready warriors had "faces...like the faces of lions, and they were as swift as the gazelles on the mountains" (1 Chron. 12:8, NAS). They were bold, poised as a lion stalking its prey, prepared to move quickly and able to adjust to tough situations. The Church will arise as a mighty army against the onslaught of the enemy as she emerges from her place of "training."

These men also were united as leaders with their leader, David. The Spirit of God prompted their chief captain, Amasai, to say to David: "Thine are we, David, and on thy side, thou son of Jesse: peace, peace be unto thee, and peace be to thine helpers; for thy God helpeth thee" (1 Chron. 12:18b). Leaders must be committed to unity and to their leader's success — not their own agenda. David's mighty men served him with great loyalty, "with an undivided heart" (1 Chron. 12:33, NAS). Such unity, according to the Scriptures, is energized by the Spirit of God.

They kept rank, not moving ahead or lagging behind, not marching in a different direction. We might say they were content with their calling — they knew the importance of maintaining their individual positions. Because they were willing to be tested and trained during the cave season, they would reign with David in his kingdom. Paul understood this process of testing. He told Timothy that "if we suffer, we shall also reign with him" (2 Tim. 2:12a).

The Church is being tested through hardship and suffering as part of her training. She must be in position to face the enemy — for he is prepared to launch a mighty counterattack against the Church.

Part Two

The Counterattack

God showed me five major, divisive, deceptive attacks that Satan has launched against the Church. These enemy attacks are real and have caused grief and misery in many churches today. But we will be comforted to know that none of their biblical counterparts, by whose names they are recognized today, won in the end. The end for believers who allow God's character to be formed in them will not be destruction. God is training His Church to be more than conquerors and enabling her to fulfill the purpose and plan of God in the earth. His Church will reflect His character before He comes again to receive His family unto Himself.

In the following chapters we will expose these attacks of the enemy against the Church. Understanding the enemy's purposes will bring hope to those who have been anticipating a move of God, but have encountered instead the grievous work of the enemy. One of Satan's first attacks will come from the spirit of Jezebel.

Three

THE SPIRIT OF JEZEBEL
Killing the Prophets

The Jezebel spirit has come against the Church in a fierce attack, intimidating many and causing much destruction. We call it the Jezebel spirit because it has taken the nature of the historical, wicked Queen Jezebel, wife of King Ahab. The Scriptures teach us much about this personality that will help us understand the attack of Satan in this area.

The first time we see Jezebel it is as a rebellious, manipulative queen who destroyed the prophets of the Lord. As Francis Frangipane writes,

> She was nearly totally responsible for corrupting

an entire nation...Jezebel is fiercely independent and intensely ambitious for pre-eminence and control. It is noteworthy that the name *Jezebel,* literally translated, means "without cohabitation." She refuses to "live together or cohabit" with anyone. Jezebel will not dwell with anyone unless she can control and dominate the relationship. When she seems submissive or "servant-like," it is only for the sake of gaining some strategic advantage. From her heart, she yields to no one. She insists on dominating and controlling every relationship.[1]

No Gender

This spirit knows no gender; it can function as well through a male as through a female personality. However, as Frangipane observes:

> The female psyche is often more vulnerable to this spirit because it desires to manipulate and control others without using physical force.[2]

It especially energizes women who are insecure, vain, jealous and dominating, having a consuming desire to control. Control is this principality's ultimate goal, and to that end it will use even sexual passion as a tool.

It is not difficult to trace the working of this Jezebel spirit in today's culture. It energizes the feminists, and is the motivator of abortion. It is especially rampant in the entertainment industry, flaunting itself in its glamor and brazen desire to seduce the minds and affections of a nation. However, we will limit our discussion to the damage it seeks to inflict on the Church.

Jezebel in the Church

The New Testament counterpart of Queen Jezebel was the Jezebel who was exposed in the church of Thyatira, as recorded in the Book of Revelation. She called herself a prophetess while seducing the servants of God to commit fornication (Rev. 2:20).

The Jezebel spirit is most often found in positions of influence and leadership. Because of its supreme desire to control, it maneuvers clandestinely until it can gain the confidence of those it seeks to influence.

In the Church, this spirit presents itself as a master of persuasion. It is strong-willed, religious and often very gifted. It may appear to be extremely loyal and willing to volunteer for special service. It may even be the spouse of a pastor. But make no mistake, the Jezebel spirit is always motivated by a character flaw that desires to control.

If this Jezebel spirit cannot actually attain to a place of leadership, it will often seek to win the confidence of those in leadership in such a way that leaders will bare their hearts to the person, telling the secrets of their lives. Then, because of the ulterior motive ruling the person with the Jezebel spirit, he or she will betray the confidence of those leaders, trying to destroy them with knowledge of their personal lives.

Dick Bernal wrote:

> You can tell the truth about someone and still

bring a curse on yourself if your motive is to hurt and discredit that individual. Truth is a two-edged sword, like a surgeon's knife. It can cut to heal, or like an enemy's sword, it can cut to kill.[3]

The Jezebel spirit seeks to kill the true servant of God in any way possible.

Our Defense Against Jezebel

Jezebel is not comfortable in a church where the Holy Spirit is given pre-eminence. Jezebel cringes when Jesus is exalted and worshipped. Repentance is greatly feared by one with a Jezebel spirit. He or she may feign repentance, but it is just to protect their influence. The Jezebel spirit knows that true repentance brings the presence of Jesus, cleanses the Church and establishes it in purity and power thus defeating the usurping control of the Jezebel spirit.

This spirit hates humility, always flaunts itself and seeks for attention. Though at times it pretends to be a self-sacrificing servant, its ulterior motive is for personal gain — to secure a place of influence and control.

It also hates prayer. Jezebel's control over Christians is ripped out of her hands by true intercessory prayer, setting Christians free while crippling this wicked spirit.

As surely as Jehu's horse trampled Queen Jezebel and destroyed her (2 Kin. 9:33), we destroy the spirit of Jezebel as we seek humility and a servant's heart, giving the Holy Spirit His rightful place in our lives and churches. Our greatest corporate and personal defense against the spirit of Jezebel is to cultivate the nature of Jesus in our hearts.

Jezebel and the Prophets

The Scriptures record that Queen Jezebel destroyed the prophets of the Lord (1 Kin. 18:4). The Jezebel spirit hates prophets, for true prophets speak against it. It wars against the prophetic message of God that condemns its rebellion and idolatry. The prophetic anointing brings exposure and defeat to the wickedness of Jezebel.

Ultimately, Jezebel's hatred is against God. The servants of God become the target of its hatred. This spirit hates the grace God lavishes upon His servants — even when they fail. It hates the holiness and purity of heart that God gives to those who serve Him.

By contrasting the Jezebel spirit with the spirit of Elijah, God's true prophet, we can better understand it. Elijah was sent to expose and confront the wickedness of Jezebel and her idolatrous worship of Baal. Again, it is Frangipane who describes these two spiritual counterparts for us:

> Is Elijah bold? Jezebel is brazen. Is Elijah ruthless toward evil? Jezebel is vicious toward righteousness. Does Elijah speak of the ways and words of God? Jezebel is full of systems of witchcraft and words of deceit.[4]

They represent the two kingdoms of light and darkness which cannot co-exist. That is the reason Jezebel threatened the life of Elijah. His demonstration of the power of God on Mount Carmel brought fire from heaven and turned a nation to serve the true God (1 Kin. 18).

Elijah and Jezebel Today

The war between the Elijah spirit and the Jezebel spirit continues to rage today. As God restores true prophetic anointing to the Church, and prophets call for righteousness and service to God, we can expect the wicked, idolatrous Jezebel spirit to be exposed. It exalts its rebellion through feminism; the murder of innocent, unborn children; and by causing God's servants to fall to immorality. It demands confrontation with the spirit of Elijah. And it is the spirit of Elijah calling for repentance and raising up prophets that will defeat the spirit of Jezebel.

Restoring Prophecy to the Church

The goal of this Jezebel spirit is to attack the purpose of God for restoring the true prophetic voice to the Church. Historical Jezebel was an idolatrous queen whose intent was to kill the true prophets of God and shut up the voice of prophecy. The Jezebel spirit is trying to do the same thing today. It will use any means to silence the voice of the prophets and to thwart the prophetic anointing to which God is calling the Church.

Five Realms of Prophecy in the Church

God is presently restoring the true voice of prophecy to the Church to strengthen and establish her in His purposes. True prophecy is the divine ability to perceive, predict, proclaim and prepare for the future. Prophecy in the Old Testament is depicted as both human activity and divine activity. God is the source of the prophetic message. Human vessels become the channel for relating that message to the people for whom the message is given.

In the New Testament, prophecy is further defined by the Greek word *propheteia,* which means "the speaking forth of the mind and counsel of God."[5] It is a declaration from God that could include prediction of the future as well as proclamation of divine realities.

In summary, we can say that prophecy is a supernatural utterance by which God communicates to people His mind and purpose, using a Spirit-filled individual as His mouthpiece.

The Scriptures also teach that the "testimony of Jesus is the spirit of prophecy" (Rev. 19:10). That holds much greater significance than a mere pseudo-exhortation that some call prophecy. It refers to the voice of our Lord Jesus Himself being heard in the Church. God wants to speak to His people today through the prophetic voice, giving Jesus His proper place in the Church.

There are at least five ways that the prophetic voice is expressed in the Church.

1. Preaching.

Paul declared that "it pleased God by the foolishness of preaching to save them that believe" (1 Cor. 1:21b). God has ordained to save the world through prophetic declaration of the truth of the Scriptures. Unfortunately, not everyone who stands behind a pulpit speaks with a prophetic anointing. But God does use human vessels who are yielded to the Holy Spirit to preach the Word with a prophetic anointing. Believers should be able to hear what the Spirit is saying to the

Church today through the present, freshly anointed, living Word of God.

2. *The office of the prophet.*

The voice of prophecy should be heard through the office of the prophet on whom the mantle of prophecy rests. According to the Scriptures, prophets are placed in the body of Christ to speak forth God's Word (Eph. 4:11). They are a vital part of equipping the Church.

3. *The gift of prophecy.*

Prophecy should be heard through believers who are willing to exercise the gift of prophecy, one of the gifts of the Holy Spirit (1 Cor. 12:10). The Scriptures give clear guidelines for the proper use of all the gifts of the Holy Spirit.

4. *Music.*

Prophecy should flow through music. We ought to hear God speak through Spirit-filled musicians worshipping God with their music. Some of the greatest prophecies I have heard came through musicians prophesying on their instruments and singing the song of the Lord. I have heard the Bridegroom sing to the bride, and I also have heard the bride sing back to her heavenly Bridegroom. I am part of a church where music is often a beautiful prophetic expression.

5. Prayer and Bible reading.

A fifth realm of prophecy includes praying prophetically and reading the Scriptures with a prophetic anointing that applies them to a present need or situation. Everyone who is filled with the Holy Spirit should learn to become a yielded channel for Him to flow through in prayer and Scripture reading. As we learn to pray according to the will of God, and allow the Word of God to live in our hearts, we will walk in revelation under a prophetic anointing.

The more we allow prophetic ministry to develop in our lives and churches, the less place we will give to the Jezebel spirit.

Tolerating Jezebel

A tolerance for Jezebel begins in our own inner sanctuary — and it is there it must be defeated. We need to ask God for the zeal of an uncompromising Jehu who cried out: "What peace, so long as the harlotries of...Jezebel and her witchcrafts are so many?" (2 Kin. 9:22, NAS). God used Jehu to destroy Jezebel.

We need to be compassionate toward people who are captured by the Jezebel spirit. But like Jehu, we offer no mercy, no hope for reform and no sympathy whatsoever to this demonic spirit. We dare not live for our own comfort while her harlotries and witchcraft are rampant in our land. As we stand with God, His judgments will come forth to destroy the Jezebel spirit.

The End of Jezebel's Witchcrafts

In the attack of the Jezebel spirit against the Church, we have seen people rise up with an idolatrous desire to rule and to shut up the true spirit of prophecy in the Church. Satan doesn't want us to hear God's voice; he knows that if we hear it, we will be part of what God is going to do in the earth. So he sent the Jezebel spirit to try to shut the mouth of the prophets.

Many times this spirit works to destroy the credibility of true prophets, and to discourage them from a desire to speak for God any longer. Elijah was tormented by Jezebel's witchcraft after his triumph on Mount Carmel. She threatened to take his life; and he found himself in a place of despair and hopelessness, running for his life (1 Kin. 19:4). When we war against the Jezebel spirit we have to guard against demonic powers of fear and discouragement. They will cause us to be distracted from the victory God has given us.

The zeal of Jehu will enable us to war against the Jezebel spirit successfully. As we pray for this zeal we do not need to fear Jezebel's onslaught. The historical Jezebel did not win! The spirit of Jezebel was defeated at Calvary! The harlotries and witchcrafts of Jezebel will be destroyed. And as the Church puts an end to Jezebel, she will recognize another deceptive spirit of witchcraft poised to strike another blow.

Four

THE SPIRIT OF WITCHCRAFT

Witchcraft Incognito

The second great attack against the Church is from the spirit of witchcraft, closely related to the Jezebel spirit. The goal of this spirit is to dilute, subjugate and destroy biblical teaching and, subsequently, the Christian life. Because it is a deceptive spirit, many Christians suffer under its bondage without being aware of it.

The apostle Paul warns us to "Put on the whole armor of God, that we may be able to stand against the wiles [or trickery] of the devil" (Eph. 6:11). He warns us that Satan will take advantage of us if we are "ignorant of his devices" (2 Cor. 2:11).

We have no reason to fear our enemy, for the Scriptures teach us that "greater is He that is in you than He that is in the world" (1 John 4:4). However, the greatest among us is vulnerable to the attack of the enemy if we fail to recognize his tactics. Our ignorance and complacency will defeat us.

Witchcraft Defined

Witchcraft can be simply defined as the technique of manipulating supernatural forces to attain one's own ends. It may involve the use of psychic powers to project an inner force onto some person or situation. When we try to use emotional power to manipulate others we are engaging in a basic form of witchcraft.

Paul includes witchcraft in his list of the works of the flesh. He wrote:

> Now the works of the flesh are manifest, which are these; Adultery, fornication, uncleanness, lasciviousness, idolatry, *witchcraft*, hatred, variance, emulations, wrath, strife, seditions, heresies, envyings, murders, drunkenness, revelings, and such like...(Gal. 5:19-21a).

The spirit of witchcraft is a counterfeit to true spiritual authority. God gives the believer spiritual authority for the purpose of edifying other believers. But an unholy or evil spirit will counterfeit true spiritual authority by using domination, manipulation, intimidation and control over other believers. We will only be free from the power of the spirit of witchcraft when we are completely submitted to the power and authority of God.

Sources of Witchcraft

The obvious sources of satanic cults or New Age philosophy are not the only sources for the spirit of witchcraft. It can come from well meaning though deceived Christians. Even prayer, if it is motivated by desire for control or manipulation, is a work of witchcraft, with powers as real as those experienced from black magic. "Charismatic" witchcraft finds its source in gossip, political maneuvering, jealousies and envyings.

Marriage partners work it on their mates; children on parents; and even businessmen and women on customers as they scheme to make a deal. Any manipulative tactic used in order to reach a selfish end can qualify as a basic form of witchcraft. Using emotional manipulation or hype to enlist the service of others, even for the work of the Lord, is a basic form of witchcraft.

We may recognize these forms of witchcraft and refuse to be manipulated. But if we become resentful or bitter toward the person projecting these tactics toward us, the enemy has gained ground within us. He will bring discouragement, disorientation and depression as surely as if we had submitted to a controlling spirit. If the enemy can get us to respond negatively in any of these situations, we will be defeated. His strategy is to cause us to depart from exercising the fruit of the Spirit, and to combat him on his own terms — fighting anger with anger.

Satan can't cast out Satan; Jezebel can't cast out Jezebel. Fighting on the enemy's terms only increases the enemy's power.

The Scriptures teach us to overcome evil with good (Rom. 12:21). Jesus Himself gave us the divine strategy for overcoming evil: "Love your enemies, bless them that curse you, do good to them that hate you, and pray for them which despitefully use you, and persecute you" (Matt. 5:44). As we pray blessings on our enemies through the power of forgiveness, the evil power of control will be broken. By not returning evil for evil, but overcoming evil with good, we destroy the power of the enemy over our lives.

To forgive does not mean we maintain fellowship with one who is determined to use manipulation and control through the power of witchcraft. Unity will not be restored in our relationship with such people without true repentance on their part. But forgiveness will free us from bitterness and resentment, and our prayers for them will be effective for their deliverance.

Our Defense

Our greatest defense against counterfeit spiritual authority is to walk in true spiritual authority, establishing our lives on truth. Though we may seem to gain a position of influence through manipulation or self-promotion — forms of counterfeit authority — such gain will ultimately become a stumbling block to receiving a true commission from God. When God establishes us in His purpose for our lives, no man or devil can undo it. But using manipulative tactics to establish and maintain our position amounts to witchcraft.

The Scriptures are clear that we should relate to one another in love. They teach us to "be subject one to another, and be clothed with humility" (1 Pet. 5:5b). Such an attitude will protect us from the manipulative work of our flesh that desires to seek its own glory. Anything done through the power of witchcraft is doomed to failure. Though we may even justify our tactics by declaring that our goal is to build the Church, God will not bless fleshly manipulation. He will build His Church according to the working of His Spirit. Anything else is an affront to the cross and ultimately will oppose the purposes of God.

Hunger for the Supernatural

The more secularized society becomes, the more magnified the hunger of man for the supernatural. The vacuum created within man for the reality of spiritual life intensifies as society declares, "There is no God." If the spiritual void in every man is not filled with real power and authority from God, as a society we will become subject to witchcraft increasingly as we draw closer to the end of this age.

Some churches that once preached the evangelical message have not followed the move of the Spirit, becoming liberal in their theology and being deceived by New Age philosophy.

We do not have to settle for counterfeit authority or be enslaved by any form of witchcraft. As we submit our lives to God and to one another in love, He will cleanse us and set us free from every evil tendency in our flesh that would thwart the purposes of God. We can be established in God's purposes and rejoice as we see the downfall of the spirits of Jezebel and of witchcraft.

Then we will be prepared to combat still another enemy that has threatened the Church through betrayal and disloyalty — the Absalom spirit.

Five

ABSALOM'S BETRAYAL
Unresolved Offense

A bsalom, King David's son, betrayed his father by steal-
ing the hearts of the men of Israel and leading them to
revolt against their king (2 Sam. 15:1-6). The
Absalom spirit of betrayal is attacking churches today. This
spirit works through discontented or offended spiritual leaders who betray the authority of the senior pastor. They seek to
build a following of people who will support their agenda,
which is contrary to the purposes and vision of the senior pastor and the majority of the congregation. This "Absalom" will
often lead his followers out of the church, causing division
and bringing great hurt to God's anointed leadership.

Characteristics of the Absalom Spirit

Like the Jezebel spirit, the Absalom spirit likes attention and is consumed with a desire for control. It is independent and bent on self-promotion. Though Absalom feigned genuine concern for the people's problems, his deeper motivation was to undermine his father's authority and to promote himself.

Absalom's Plot

Absalom sat outside the city gates declaring his father's neglect of the people and presenting himself as the righteous judge in the land. He received the men of Israel with great affection, kissing their hands and promising them justice. The Scriptures say, "so Absalom stole the hearts of the men of Israel" (2 Sam. 15:6). When he had succeeded in positioning himself in a place of favor with the people, Absalom deceitfully asked permission of his father to let him go to Hebron to make a sacrifice. He intended to proclaim himself king while in Hebron.

The Scriptures declare how deeply this deception affected the people: "And with Absalom went two hundred men out of Jerusalem, that were called; and they went in their simplicity, and they knew not anything" (2 Sam. 15:11). So complete was his deception that those who followed him did not even realize they were part of a conspiracy against God's anointed leadership.

So today, many naive, innocent, unsuspecting people are seduced into disloyalty to their leadership by this Absalom spirit of betrayal.

The apparent cause of offense between King David and his son Absalom was the earlier murder by Absalom of his half-brother, Amnon. After the murder Absalom lived in exile for several years. Then the king allowed him to return to Jerusalem, but refused a face-to-face meeting with his son.

Finally, Absalom persuaded his father to see him. When they met, King David kissed Absalom.

This attempt at reconciliation was not complete, however, for soon after their meeting Absalom began to stand by the palace gates to greet the men of Israel who came to the king with controversies. He maligned his father to them, lamenting that there was no one to hear their matters. He suggested that it would be good if he were appointed to do so — he would bring them justice. Absalom was a prince of flattery and perverted praise, which he used to gain the favor of the people. In this calculating way he gradually stole the hearts of the men of Israel.

Absalom did not undermine his father's authority in one day. There was a long process during which Absalom became openly disloyal and divisive. For forty years he continued to criticize the king and his administration, exalting himself as the righteous man of the hour. He did not bring his disloyalty out into the open until he felt that people were loyal to him and willing to follow him.

His conspiracy was so well thought out and his deception so complete that neither the two hundred men who went with him nor King David suspected any foul play. Perhaps David was blinded by his love for his son. However, once he declared himself king at Hebron (2 Sam. 15:10), everyone became aware of the dreadful conspiracy that threatened the kingdom. Now the people were forced to make a choice between two leaders: King David, God's anointed leadership, and Absalom, the prince who had deceived them.

Supportive Leadership

The very nature of this wicked spirit of betrayal makes church leaders especially vulnerable to its working. Many times this spirit works through associate ministers and other staff members who have served in a church for twenty years or longer. Suddenly these individuals refuse to cooperate with the senior pastor.

Two main causes for their refusal are personal ambition and unresolved offenses. They become discontented in their role as supportive leadership, wanting to be number one; or they fail to resolve little offenses along the way that rise up to become a stronghold in which the enemy can work. Before long they have begun the process of betrayal, spreading their criticism and discontent to those who will listen.

People who are not willing to be led by God's true leadership are vulnerable to this deception. It is easy for an "Absalom" to win their approval of his or her criticism of the leadership. Usually, those who are influenced by the Absalom spirit attempt to usurp the true authority that God has established and set up their own kingdoms. They cannot work alongside God's leadership in a supportive role.

Such wickedness in high places can wreak havoc in the lives of people, and in the kingdom of God. Sincere believers must guard against accepting criticism against spiritual leadership, even if it comes from another leader. Do not trust a person simply because of the title or position he or she holds in the church. Be aware of the fruit they produce in their lives and in their relationships. A broken relationship should signal danger, especially when it involves an estrangement from the leader to whom God has given the authority in that church or ministry.

I have sat with pastors who were suffering because of an Absalom betrayal. They lamented: "I trusted him. I would have turned my whole church over to him." This Absalom spirit, energized by unresolved offense and the desire to be number one, has opened many otherwise qualified servants of God to deception. Because they allow themselves to be ruled by the Absalom spirit, their actions bring division and great hurt to the kingdom of God.

Second Fiddle

An orchestra leader once told me that the hardest chair to fill in the symphony is the second violinist — the "second fiddle." Though it is one of the most important positions in the whole orchestra, having much to do with the precise, harmonious sound of the music, musicians do not appreciate it. They would rather be first chair.

Unfortunately, people in supportive leadership roles in the Church sometimes express this sentiment. They plan to stay in their present position only until they get a promotion. The youth pastor, just serving his time while he waits for a better position to come along, wonders why he is not effective with the youth. The young people sense his lack of real concern for them and instinctively do not respect him because of his personal ambition. They want a pastor who cares about them, instead of someone whom they sense is using them to climb to a higher position.

We need to realize that God appoints people to areas of leadership. He enables them, by His Spirit, to fulfill certain tasks in building His church. If what you are doing now is the will of God for your life, you could do nothing more noble. Whether He has gifted you to be an associate minister, youth pastor or pianist, you should accept that appointment gratefully and be content in that role. It is a place of anointing and safety.

Some people who hold ministry positions do not want to be accountable to anyone. They refuse to accept counsel or discipline into their lives, intent on having their own ministry. They do not realize that if the ministry is "theirs," it will die and blow away. Ministries that cannot be brought under the leadership of the local church, confirmed by the apostles, prophets, pastors, evangelists and teachers that God established to guide the church, are not to be trusted. Such so-called ministry may be the result of one person's desire to rule and build his or her own reputation.

I am very grateful for ministers who are comfortable working under another minister's leadership. The test of a true leader is his or her ability to work well with another leader. you cannot truly lead if you are not first willing to be led; you cannot teach if you are not willing to be taught. Those who become offended by serving in supportive roles, or who want to be number one, are vulnerable to deception from the Absalom spirit.

Offense Defined

The word for offense in Greek is *skandalon,* from which we derive our word "scandal." It literally means "a trap-stick (bent sapling); a snare; or part of a trap set with bait to catch its victim." [1] Satan uses offense as a bait to trap us and bring us into captivity to the sins of anger, outrage, jealousy, envy, resentment, strife, bitterness, hatred and even murder. Nursing those offenses produces the fruit of a critical spirit, insulting and wounding attitudes, divisiveness, backsliding and betrayal.

Offended people can be divided into two categories: those who have been treated unjustly and those who perceive they have been treated unjustly. People in the second category are convinced they have been wronged. Though their conclusions may be drawn from inaccurate information, their misunderstanding brings on the same pangs of offense as are suffered by people who have actually been wronged.

The fruit of unresolved offense develops progressively. It begins with hurt and anger, but soon develops into hatred. It can even express itself ultimately in murder. The violence we are witnessing in the world today is evidence of the fruit of offense. It can be seen in spouse abuse and murder; domestic violence; family violence with sons and daughters killing parents and siblings killing siblings; and even in rape and incest.

Unresolved offense leads to bitterness; bitterness leads to hatred; hatred leads to wrath; and wrath often leads to murder.

Causes of Offense

Too often the cause of offense resides in our own minds. The world's mentality asserts, "My rights!" and desires to get even with those who violate them. Our pride seeks its own exaltation and refuses to forgive those who do not give us the recognition we deserve. That spirit shuts out heaven and brings deception to our hearts. If we indulge those attitudes, it won't be long until we convince ourselves that people are against us and we are justified in our criticism of them.

We also can be offended by the tests and trials of life that God allows. Unless we respond correctly, difficult circumstances which cause pain will offend. God develops His character in us through trials and tests. We will not always like the process that is required to make us Christlike. But as we submit willingly to the dealings of God we will be freed from our offended attitudes. As forgiveness works in us, the love of God will be "shed abroad in our hearts by the Holy Ghost which is given unto us" (Rom. 5:5).

Offense in the Church

Offense may be the strongest weapon the enemy uses to divide the Church. According to Jesus, we cannot live in this world without experiencing offense. He declared: "It is impossible but that offenses will come: but woe unto him, through whom they come!" (Luke 17:1). Though we are promised that offenses will come, it is not the offense itself, but our reaction to it, that determines our future.

There are no walls that we can build against offense so that we will never be hurt. God will help us to respond correctly when offenses come. As we put aside our pride, we can humbly forgive those who offend us. God can change hurtful situations into blessings that will result in godly character, making us more humble and less self-centered.

Jesus said, "And blessed is he, whosoever shall not be offended in me" (Luke 7:23). Though we would not admit readily to being offended with Jesus, to nurse offense against

His people is to be offended with Him. It is vital to walk in forgiveness with our brothers and sisters in Christ, keeping short accounts, so that we will not be ensnared by the devastating consequences of nursing offense. Jesus lives in the hearts of our brothers and sisters. The Scriptures tell us, "Inasmuch as ye have done it unto one of the least of these my brethren, ye have done it unto me" (Matt. 25:40).

Biblical Response to Offense

The Old Testament records the history of Joseph, the favorite son of Jacob, who was mistreated by his brothers, thrown into a pit and sold into slavery. He spent some of the best years of his life in exile from his family and country, and then suffered an unjust imprisonment. Yet he did not harbor offense or nurse a grudge against his brothers. He forgave them and declared that it was God who had allowed his "misfortune" so that he could help to save their lives in the end (Gen. 45:5).

He didn't know God was preparing him for rulership. He didn't know that these circumstances were ordained to shape his character. But he submitted to the will of God in every situation and enjoyed the presence of God in his life.

Jesus clearly taught us how to be reconciled to someone who has offended us (see Matthew 18). We must be willing to communicate with the offender, going to them in a conciliatory attitude to be reconciled. We dare not suppress hurt feelings, for those feelings will develop into hatred. In our homes, marriage partners need to resolve offenses quickly. The Word of God instructs, "let not the sun go down upon your wrath" (Eph. 4:26). Following this admonition will keep us from nursing grudges until they grow into hatred and lead to divorce.

The apostle Paul gives a beautiful revelation of love that is free from from unresolved offense:

> Love is patient, love is kind, and is not jealous;
> love does not brag and is not arrogant, does not
> act unbecomingly; it does not seek its own, is not
> provoked, does not take into account a wrong
> suffered (1 Cor. 13:4-5, NAS).

According to the Scriptures, the way to get over offense is to show love to the offender. That is why Jesus taught us to love our enemies. He knew the good it would do for us, setting us free from the trap of offense, as well as affecting our enemies' lives for good.[2]

Proper Perspective

A proper perspective will enable a believer to walk through a trial victoriously. Proclaim: "Satan, you think you laid a trap for me, but it won't catch me. Without my Father's permission, this trial would not have happened. He permitted it, even if He didn't promote it. He knew I would make it through victoriously if I walked with Him. And He also knew I would be more like Him when the trial was over."

Jesus was rejected, spat upon and called by evil names. He was forsaken by the men He loved the most. They deserted Him in the time of His greatest trial. Judas betrayed Him, Peter denied Him and they all forsook Him. If we desire to be like Jesus, we must respond to our painful situations as He did to His. Though He was mistreated, He never became offended.

Only our wrong attitudes, reactions and refusal to forgive will hinder God's working in our lives. No person or situation can take us out of the will of God.

Absalom in the Church

We have seen how unresolved offense can lead to serious sin. It can open us to the deception of the Absalom spirit of betrayal. As Absalom stole the hearts of the men of Israel, so these flatterers learn to speak in such a way in the church that unsuspecting Christians begin to admire them. This admiration produces a spiritual pride in the deceived "Absaloms," who begin to believe they are more spiritual than their leaders.

Then a competitive spirit takes over, and "Absalom" begins to misrepresent the decisions of the leadership and the direction they are taking. He (or she) sows strife and division and draws a group of people to himself. His followers feed off his critical spirit.

After that, there arises a bold conspiracy. The "Absalom" justifies the actions of his group by focusing on the minor issues with which he found fault in the leadership. Usually his accusations are not related to false doctrine or blatant sin within the leadership. Rather, he magnifies the imperfections or human traits of the leader.

Soon "Absalom" leads a naive splinter group out to start a new church built on the foundation of offense. Since it is not built on the right foundation it cannot prosper. If the root of a tree is bad, the whole tree will be bad. So it is with every church that is founded on an Absalom spirit. It will be full of rebellion and disloyalty and will suffer continual church splits. God's judgment is on the rebellious church.

Testimony of Fellowship Restored

I know a minister who became the pastor of a church in California that seemed dead to the presence of God. No matter how they changed their worship, or how he preached, the Lord did not move among the people. This pastor determined to find the cause for the lack of God's presence in the church.

One night, while meeting with the board of the church, the pastor asked, "Can you tell me how this church was founded?"

"Why do you need to know that?" the chairman of the board asked.

"I want to know why God's presence is not here. There must be something wrong in the church," he replied. "Do you know how this church was birthed?"

The board replied that the church began as a split from another church more than twenty years earlier. They related that the mother church now had a new pastor, different leadership and many new members who were not even aware of the history of the church split.

"But we cannot expect to experience the presence of God in our church until we reconcile this long-standing offense," my pastor friend responded.

Taking the board of the church with him, this pastor went to the pastor of the mother church. "You don't know us or our history," he stated. "But our church began as a split off your church. We have come to be reconciled with your church and to forgive the offenses of long-standing between these churches."

The pastors and board members of these two churches prayed together and established a bond of love and fellowship with each other. After that simple confession and act of reconciliation, God's presence returned to my friend's church as the Holy Spirit began to move among the people.

A Warning

God spoke a startling message to me one night as I was ministering in a church in North Carolina. He declared: "I will not, I will not, I will not allow anyone who touches My plan, My program, My prophets or My prophecy to be a part of, or participate in, the next move of God."

I immediately recognized the book of Jude in outline form in that statement. He had mentioned four of the seven steps that led the Church into apostasy. I realized that there are sins committed against God that are much worse than sins we commit against our fellow man. It is not a light matter to be involved in criticism or betrayal of an anointed servant of God.

The End of Absalom

When we try to overthrow God's purposes by touching God's anointed leadership we can expect to suffer the consequences. Absalom suffered a humiliating and untimely death, while King David was restored to his throne as the rightful king. God's true anointed leadership, though not perfect, will triumph over the Absalom spirit as these anointed leaders place themselves in God's hands as King David did. As believers and supportive leadership, we need to guard our hearts so that we are not guilty of harboring personal ambition or unresolved offense that will deceive us and make us vulnerable to the Absalom spirit. And we need to guard our relationships, not allowing anyone to undermine God's leadership by criticism. Otherwise, we could become a part of Absalom's tragic end.

We need to be prepared to guard our hearts and relationships against the attack of Absalom. But we must set a guard around our very minds as the enemy offers to open them to freedom, but instead causes great harm and emotional bondage to those who fall victim to the spirit of pseudo-counseling.

Six

THE SPIRIT OF PSEUDO-COUNSELING

Destroying the Believers

A fourth attack against the Church came in the form of a pseudo-counseling spirit. This spirit has invaded the Church from the secular world, and is the most detrimental force I have ever seen claim to be Christian. Raising its head in many of our charismatic churches, as well as in other denominations, it is a humanistic counseling approach for what is called post traumatic memory syndrome I have personally witnessed the tragic results of this form of counseling, watching it wreck homes, destroy family relationships and split churches.

I believe in spiritual counseling. I believe God places people in churches to counsel. A true counselor is one who knows

The Counselor — our Lord Jesus — and who is guided by the Holy Spirit. A counselor who knows the Word of God, functions in the spiritual gifts of knowledge and wisdom and follows the direction of the Holy Spirit will give sound counsel. Any other source of counsel should not be trusted.

Counterfeit Spiritual Counsel

Counseling for post traumatic memory syndrome has found its way into the church counseling chamber. I have personally talked with pastors and other people who have been victims of this counseling approach, often perpetrated upon them by unqualified counselors.

Using this approach, someone sitting under the banner of "Christian counselor" suggests false ideas and accusations to the person they are counseling regarding something someone has done to them in the past. These accusations later work on that person's power of recall until he (or she) "remembers" the past negative circumstance the counselor suggested, believing it is coming from his own memory. It is projected to the counselee's memory initially by the counselor, then retrieved from the counselee as fact.

The negative circumstance in his memory is then blamed for his present emotional problems. The counselee is instructed to face his offender, telling that person how the remembered offense has damaged his psyche and caused his present unhappy emotional state.

I understand that there has been much child abuse, molestation and other evil perpetrated on the young. But I believe this type of counseling is not the answer to help someone cope with those past problems, real or imagined.

When I went to prayer and asked my Father about this extreme counseling approach, He gave me one sentence that satisfied my spirit. He said, "My daughter, if Calvary — the death of My Son — satisfied the heart of God regarding sin, why will it not satisfy the mind of man?"

The power of Jesus' blood is just as real today as it was the day He died. He is the only One who can transform us and heal us from the negative consequences of our sinful nature and past hurts. If the efficacious, vicarious, mediatorial, substitutionary work of Calvary is not enough to redeem us from our sins and heal our psyches, we have no other remedy.

These Christian pseudo-counselors say by their actions that the blood of Calvary isn't the whole answer for redemption. They believe the Church does not offer what we need for complete spiritual healing. Though psychology has discovered some principles that can be helpful in understanding problems, my concern is when psychological counseling discovers the problem but denies the remedy found only in Christ. The psyche cannot restore itself. The Scriptures declare that God gives a sound mind, a supernatural work of redemption. Those who defend this extreme form of counseling insist their spiritual counseling can take a person back into the womb or to a childhood experience that is having an emotional effect on that person today. Yet, if they fail to bring that person to the cross of Christ, they are powerless to effect healing in that life.

I know a woman who suffered greatly at the hands of such a counselor. Her counselor said her emotional problems were caused by her father, who had molested her when she was too young to remember. My friend had a godly father who could not have conceived of such wickedness against his daughter.

Yet, believing the counselor's conclusion, this woman went to her father's home to "resolve" this offense.

When she told her godly father that she had discovered his molestation of her as a child, he stared at her in disbelief. Shortly after her announcement to him of his "offense," he dropped dead. The shock of such a wicked accusation coming from his daughter had killed him.

That is only one illustration of the destruction this ungodly counseling spirit has caused. Where counseling for post traumatic memory syndrome has been practiced in churches, it has created divisions and resulted in church splits. I know of a church in Dallas, one of the best churches in this country, where three hundred people walked out as a result of being deceived by this pseudo-counseling. Church leaders taught that the blood of Christ and the cross were not sufficient to cleanse sins of the past.

"Self" Heresy

I attended a recent conference of pastors and leaders who spent hours sharing the damage this pseudo-counseling spirit has done in their churches. The whole premise for this type of counseling is rooted in the humanistic philosophy that mankind is basically good — it is the bad things that happen to us that make us miserable. Psychologists have done their best to get us to esteem, love and honor ourselves. The result of this humanistic teaching is a "self" heresy. It has created a doctrine in the church today that is elevating self.

Christians who offer counseling for post traumatic memory syndrome reject the doctrine of sanctification which teaches us to bring our self-life to the cross and exchange it for the life of Christ. In this way, they exchange the cross of Christ for the "couch."

Jesus taught us that if we want to follow Him, we must deny self and take up our cross (Matt. 16:24). The Scriptures clearly teach us to exchange our self-life with its carnal thinking, warped emotions and rebellious wills for the new life we find in Christ. We are to take up our cross daily so that we can learn to walk in newness of life. Deliverance from the sinful self-life will come by choosing the cross. Just listening to counsel — even godly counsel — won't do it.

It is true that we are to love ourselves, for Jesus taught us to love our neighbors as we love ourselves. But self-absorption — the inevitable result of "self" heresy — keeps us from loving our neighbors. To love ourselves in a godly sense means we will place our carnal self-life on the cross of Calvary. We will seek help from Christians who minister to us through the anointing of the Holy Spirit and the Word of God. We will find deliverance from our sinfulness through the blood of Jesus. As the Christ-life flows through us it will set us free to love others.

Calvary settles it all. We don't have to go around with bandages on our minds or emotions for fifteen years after we are saved. Children wear bandages to get attention. I believe some immature Christians look for someone else who will agree with their complaint because they think the Church doesn't give them enough attention or meet their needs. They are not serious about bringing their need to the cross to find deliverance. Such immature conduct makes them vulnerable targets for the pseudo-counselor.

As we mature in God we will discover that our own needs for attention are met as we learn to meet the needs of others.

Growing up in Christ will keep us from being victims of the pseudo-counselor's false pity which brings destruction rather than healing to our souls.

God Forgets

As I knelt one night by a little girl who was repenting of her sins and receiving Jesus as her Savior, I said, "Honey, your sins have just been forgiven. Never again will God ever remember your sins."

Then I added one more sentence that the Church world often says: "Satan may drag up your sins," I continued. "But God will never remember them against you anymore."

In that moment my heavenly Father rebuked me.

"Daughter," I heard my Father say, "when did the devil become omniscient? How does the devil know what I can't remember? If I forgot it, what makes you think his memory exceeds mine?" As I listened He continued firmly, "Furthermore, how can he put his hands beneath the precious blood of Jesus? I put the sins of a repentant sinner under the blood, blotting them out forever. The devil cannot touch them — you are in error!"

Recognizing my error, I replied, "Yes, Lord."

"But you have a question?" he continued.

"Yes, I do," I answered. "Why do we remember our own sins?"

"If my people would learn to keep their mouths shut about their past sins," my Father responded, "the devil wouldn't have so much information to feed back to them."

Too often we talk about what we used to do and discuss the past of others. By doing this we inform the devil, giving him a weapon to hurl at us — the memory of our sins. By God's grace we can push the "delete memory" button and replace the past with Paul's admonition: "whatsoever things are true, whatsoever things are honest, whatsoever things are just, whatsoever things are pure, whatsoever things are lovely, whatsoever things are of good report; if there be any virtue, and if there be any praise, think on these things" (Phil. 4:8).

The End of the Pseudo-counseling Spirit

> But when He, the Spirit of truth, comes, He will guide you into all the truth; for He will not speak on His own initiative, but whatever He hears, He will speak; and He will disclose to you what is to come (John 16:13, NAS).

When He — the blessed Holy Spirit — is come, we have no need for ungodly counselors anymore.

There is a Comforter — a divine Helper, the blessed Holy Spirit — who speaks healing to our past in a moment. It doesn't take Him ten sessions to dig up our past. By yielding to His supernatural work of cleansing, we will be truly delivered, set free to love and serve God. Do not be deceived by the pseudo-counseling spirit. As we yield to the Holy Spirit's work of redemption, and to the ministry of a godly counselor when needed, we will find the healing and restoration we need to serve effectively in the body of Christ.

But there remains one more enemy to defeat. And this one has targeted the destruction of the life of Christ within the Church.

Seven

THE PHARISAICAL SPIRIT
Hostility That Kills

The last attack against the Church that we have seen comes through the pharisaical spirit. This spirit is filled with a deadly hostility. The pharisaical spirit killed Abel, crucified Jesus, stoned Stephen and tried to do away with Paul. Its target is still the life of Christ, and it will try to destroy the Christ-life that dwells within believers today.

By nature the pharisaical spirit hates the grace of God but loves legalism. The Pharisees rejected Jesus as He preached the good news of the gospel to the poor. Though He was the chief cornerstone on which God was building His kingdom, they rejected Him for their own interpretation of the Old Testa-

Testament and for their religious traditions. Through these traditions, while receiving the praise of men they could manipulate and control the lives of people for their own benefit.

When they tried to judge Jesus according to their traditions, He challenged the legalism they held so dear. Upholding their laws was more important to them than building a relationship with the Living Word. Jesus Christ — the only hope for true salvation — became a stumbling block to them. Salvation that was freely given would rob them of the satisfaction of earning their reward through legalistic rituals.

Simeon prophesied of their dilemma when he held the baby Jesus in his arms in the temple: "Behold this child is set for the fall and rising again of many in Israel; and for a sign which shall be spoken against" (Luke 2:34b). The Prince of Peace, sent to reconcile the world to Himself, brought a sword of division to those to whom He was sent — the house of Israel (Matt. 15:24). They loved their darkness and refused to come to the Light.

Jesus' miracles threatened the Pharisees' popularity and power with the people, for they could not do what He did. Jesus revealed a gospel of love and forgiveness, but the Pharisees required obedience to rules that superseded the Scriptures, and insisted their rules were the only way to righteousness. Theirs was a salvation by works — Jesus offered salvation through repentance, worship and a personal relationship with Him.

The Pharisee and Worship

The pharisaical spirit militates against true worship and relationship with God. But Jesus warned them: "Woe unto you...Pharisees, hypocrites! for ye shut up the kingdom of heaven against men, for ye neither go in yourselves, neither suffer ye them that are entering to go in" (Matt. 23:13). Worship was the central issue the first time the pharisaical spirit was manifested. Adam's son, Cain, the first murderer in the world, manifested a pharisaical spirit toward his brother, Abel.

Cain became angry with Abel when God accepted Abel's offering of worship but did not accept his own. The New Testament tells us, "by faith Abel offered unto God a more excellent sacrifice than Cain, by which he obtained witness that he was righteous" (Heb. 11:4a). Cain hated Abel because his righteousness was accepted by God.

God spoke to Cain, asking him why he was angry, and assuring him that if he did well, he would be accepted. He told him also that if he did not do well, sin was lying at the door (see Gen. 4:3-7). God gave Cain an opportunity to repent, but Cain persisted in his own way and hated his brother, who had pleased God.

That first murder was typical of the Pharisees' desire to kill Jesus, the Righteous One. The Pharisees hated Jesus because they had made an idol of religion and had rejected the true righteousness of the Scriptures. Jesus said to them: "You search the Scriptures, because you think that in them you have eternal life; and it is these that bear witness of Me; and you are unwilling to come to Me, that you may have life" (John 5:40, NAS). They preferred honor from one another and rule by their traditions to the life that Jesus offered them.

Jesus was tolerant of sinners who came to Him, but He had no tolerance for the Pharisee. The Pharisees and doctors of the law were the only ones for whom He did not have one kind word. He didn't bless them — He pronounced woe upon them, calling them whited sepulchres (Matt. 23:27), and murderers like their father, the devil (John 8:44). His evaluation proved to be correct, for they were the ones who later crucified Him. Pilate, a pagan ruler, observed "that for envy" they had condemned Jesus to death (Matt. 27:17-18).

Pharisaical Spirit in the Church

People who are ruled by a pharisaical spirit today love the praises of men. They are very concerned about position and honor. They insist on ruling over people with their traditions and laws. They are not impressed with the humble way that Jesus came, healing the sick and feeding the multitudes. They are content to receive glory to themselves for their feigned righteousness.

The pharisaical spirit is one of the greatest abominations that has ever invaded the Church. It masquerades as "super-spiritual." There is no such thing as super-spiritual — for no one can have too much of God. But there are many people who have too much of religion. To be "super-religious" is not the same as being spiritual. Those who allow the nature of Christ to be seen in their lives are truly spiritual.

As with the other five spirits mentioned earlier, people who are ruled by a pharisaical spirit despise authority and true leadership. They are too "spiritual" to be corrected. These religious people do not want to be planted in a local church. They cannot flow in unity with God's anointed leadership. They exalt their own opinions and become bitter, critical and censorious of others. They live as an island unto themselves, exalting themselves above the humble spirit of our Lord.

The intent of the pharisaical spirit is to kill the Christ-life in each one of us. The first place to look for this spirit is within our own self-life. We resist the idea that our flesh is religious. But without the fullness of the Christ life in us, it is simply human nature to be religious. But as we humble ourselves to receive the Word of God joyfully, we will learn to guard against the characteristics of the pharisaical spirit we are describing.

In church life, the pharisaical spirit seeks the "chief seats" (Matt. 23:6). This spirit tries to take pre-eminence, defying the humble Christ-like spirit. It will seek attention one way or another. Although it can't crucify Christ again, it will try to keep Him from living in the Church. Its motivation is to put to death the Christ life wherever it is found. I would rather deal with the most degraded sinner than have someone pharisaical in my church.

Thy Word Is Truth

The enemy and his evil spirits were waging a battle to keep God's truth from the people when the Lord Himself walked the earth. That battle has continued down through history even to this day. Satan's attempt to keep the Word of God out of the hands of the common people was the great spiritual battleground of the Reformation. Satan knows that revelation of God's Word to our hearts will result in his overthrow as the prince of the air. For this reason the Lord declared that the poor would have the gospel preached to them (Matt. 11:5). As they receive Him they are set free from the tyranny of the devil and the power of sin.

Today, many spiritual leaders cannot respond to the Word of God because they are bound by their own doctrines and traditions. Radical obedience to the Word is required in order to release the living waters from which revival springs. True revival is a revolution against the prevailing principalities and powers of the enemy. The pharisaical spirit is Satan's most powerful weapon in this battle, masquerading as the protector of legitimate truth.

The Pharisees were given primary responsibility for maintaining the integrity of the written Word through centuries of copying and re-copying. We owe them much for their diligence. But in their zeal to protect the Scriptures from abuse, the Pharisees implemented a system of interpretation based more on their own traditions than on the actual text. Their love of these traditions caused them to reject and even persecute the One who was the personified Word of God.

The pharisaical spirit esteems the written Word above the living Word. It worships the Book of the Lord instead of the Lord of the Book.

The modern counterparts of the Pharisees of Jesus' day still try to protect the Scriptures from doctrinal abuse. But in their zeal they have created an intricate system of interpretation which may serve as some protection for the integrity of their doctrine, but which also limits radically any further revelation for those who want to obey the truth. They fight for the truth, yet miss the moving of the Holy Spirit during revival because His revelation transcends their doctrinal understanding.

Everyone who loves the truth desires sound doctrine also. Sound doctrine, though important, is not meant to be an end in itself. Adopting such a position results in arguments among brethren and divisions in the body of Christ. Sound doctrine is meant to teach us how to be conformed to the image of

Christ. It enables us to determine the will of God so that we can obey Him.

When we stand before the judgment seat of Christ, we will be judged according to our relationship with Jesus and for our service to Him — not according to how accurate our doctrine was. Our motivation, attitudes and availability to the will of God are the criteria by which we will be judged.

It is possible to memorize the entire Bible and still not know the truth. Truth is a Person. The Pharisees loved the Scriptures more than they loved the God of the Scriptures. Many today fall prey to this same deception. We cannot love God without loving His Word. But it is possible to elevate the written Word above God Himself, making an idol out of the Scriptures. If that happens, we allow the Scriptures to supplant our relationship with God.

Personal relationship — this priceless gift of the Lord to His people — is the truth that will set us free from the bondage of legalism. Christians should search the Scriptures to find the God of the Scriptures. One of the greatest tragedies today is that we read into the Word according to a doctrine or tradition that someone has taught us, instead of reading out what the Holy Spirit wants to reveal to us.

The End of the Pharisee

Jesus Himself declared the end of the Pharisees in the great Magna Carta of the gospel — the Beatitudes. He warned:

> For I say unto you, That except your righteous-
> ness shall exceed the righteousness of the scribes

and Pharisees, ye shall in no case enter into the
kingdom of heaven (Matt. 5:20).

The pharisaical spirit will never enter the kingdom of
heaven. We must guard our hearts against this wicked spirit or
lose the kingdom of God.

Jesus condemned the Pharisees publicly, crying,

> Woe unto you, scribes and Pharisees, hypocrites!
> for ye shut up the kingdom of heaven against
> men: for ye neither go in yourselves, neither suffer
> ye them that are entering to go in (Matt. 23:13).

It was the pharisaical spirit that killed Jesus. That same
spirit is determined to destroy the Christ that lives in you.
The Church cannot co-exist with it. As a Spirit-filled believer,
stand and declare boldly, "His house will be a house of prayer,
purity and holiness! I command you pharisaical spirit to get
out! You will not rule my church. I will not give you a place
of leadership here!"

We do not have to be victims of this deception if we
choose to submit to the truth of God in obedience to His will.

A Glorious Church

None of these deceiving spirits that invade the Church
will be victorious in the end. That's good news! As we yield to
the Spirit of God and refuse to compromise we will not be
vulnerable to any of these five marauding spirits at work in
our world today. God is faithful to reveal His truth to our
hearts and deliver us from these evils.

God will have a glorious Church without spot or wrinkle — a beautiful bride for His Son. It is time for the Church to come out of the cave, into the light of day. As she emerges, she is going to be different from who she was when she went into the cave. Her heart will have been circumcised from the love of the world and of self, and will be filled with love for God alone. The Church will fulfill His purposes in the earth as He comes to fill her with His glory.

Set free from her cave experience, the Church will then be ready to overcome the external hindrances to revival.

Eight

HINDERING CONCEPTS TO REVIVAL
Cleansing the Church

As I have waited expectantly for the revival God showed me in my vision of 1963, the Holy Spirit has deeply impressed upon me that the Church needs cleansing from at least five hindering concepts in order to be a part of the coming revival.

Denominationalism

A denomination is a class or society of individuals supporting a system of principles and called by the same name. As long as a denomination remains open to the life of Jesus, it is not harmful. It can be an instrument of God. However,

79

when denominational doctrines are taught with dogmatic finality, greater streams of truth that would flow through it are limited.

Elitism, legalism and judgmental attitudes almost always result from such dogma. Such denominationalism, established upon man's ideologies and dogmas, obscures the true Church that Christ is building.

The purpose of a denomination is the same as that of scaffolding that is erected during a building process. However, scaffolding was not designed to obscure permanently the structure being built. When that happens, it has lost its useful purpose and become a hindrance. It needs to be removed in order for the real building to be seen. For the life of Christ to be seen in the Church, the scaffolding of denominationalism must be removed.

I recall the words of God during my vision of the hydro-electric plant. When God was ready to pull the switch that would bring revival, He declared: "This time, no man, no devil, no demon and no denomination will ever dam it up again." We can surely anticipate this wonderful liberty through which the truth of God will flow.

Human Tradition

Webster defines tradition as "an inherited, established or customary pattern of thought, action or behavior; the handing down of information, beliefs and customs by word of mouth or by example from one generation to another without written instruction." [1]

The Pharisees asked Jesus, "Why do thy disciples transgress the tradition of the elders? for they wash not their hands when they eat bread" (Matt. 15:2). Tradition was more important to them than the Word of God.

Jesus was critical of and even repudiated the oral tradition, concluding that the oral decrees of the elders were wholly of human origin (Mark 7:6-13). And Paul declared that he was more exceedingly zealous of the traditions of his fathers until "it pleased God...to reveal his Son in me" (Gal. 1:14-16). He was delivered from devout loyalty to an intense religious system when Christ was revealed in him.

Because man's carnal mind has interpreted many of the Scriptures in the Church today, the Holy Spirit, the divine Teacher who wrote the Book, has not been allowed to reveal truth to our spirits. As a result we have developed religious practices that are "comfort zones" to our church mentality. Failing to "rightly divide the Word of God" (1 Tim. 2:15), instead we have read it according to the instruction of men.

Peter reminds us that we "were not redeemed with perishable things like silver and gold, "from your futile way of life inherited from your forefathers" (1 Pet. 1:18, NAS). Tradition is not the source of our redemption — the Word of God is. The Spirit of Truth will teach us what truth means and will deliver us from religious tradition. God's Word is the final "yea and amen." It alone will be fulfilled to the letter as God intended.

I believe God is creating in the hearts of believers a new hunger and thirst for His Word. As we search the Scriptures and seek God with all our hearts, He has promised to satisfy our hunger and quench our thirst. Revelation will increase as we find Him as our wisdom. Then the true Church will emerge, filled with the life-giving waters of the Holy Spirit.

Prejudice

Unreasonable biases, judgments or opinions, held in disregard of facts, breed suspicion, intolerance or hatred and have no place in Christ's Church. Whether it is against race, gender, sect, class or status, prejudice will keep us from hearing and receiving the truth of God as revealed by the Holy Spirit.

Paul declared, "after that faith is come" (Gal. 3:25), in Christ our prejudicial distinctions do not exist (Gal. 3:28). He admonished Timothy "that you guard and keep [these rules] without personal prejudice or favor, doing nothing from partiality" (1 Tim 5:21, AMP).

In his christological epistles,[2] Paul teaches us to live in an attitude of humility; esteeming one another above ourselves; loving one another fervently; and looking out for the interests of others. In His great love chapter he defines God's love as longsuffering, kind and seeking not its own (1 Cor. 13). This is a picture of the true Church of Christ, delivered from the destructive power of prejudice.

Culture

Perhaps nothing is more basic to our natural thinking than culture — the concepts, habits, arts, institutions and refinements of thought, manners, and taste that characterize our native environment. These traits seem "right" to us. That is why some missionaries have exported more culture than Christ-life as they have attempted to conform others to their own lifestyle.

We have to be delivered from our bondage to culture in

order to allow Christ to move in us and through us to any culture. He brings a new and higher way of life that transcends the limitations of culture. He will help us establish a lifestyle within our individual cultures that is free from the sins of those cultures.

Many of Paul's teachings addressed issues of culture. He taught the necessity of moving our spiritual focus from the external cultural issues to the greater moral and ethical issues of our heart attitudes toward God, our fellowman and ourselves. Living godly lives in a sinful culture was difficult for Christians in Paul's day, as it is in our world. People were often more concerned with externals than with true issues of godly character and motivation.

As we learn to embrace a lifestyle without compromise with the external, we will be able to live a godly life in our sinful cultures. We can learn to live *in* this world without being part of it. Then we will be salt and light to those around us.

Purity of heart will establish godly priorities in every area of life as God's kingdom of righteousness, peace and joy in the Holy Ghost (Rom. 14:17) comes to us.

Customs

A custom is "a long-established practice considered as unwritten law; a uniform practice by common consent of a society to such an extent that it has taken on the force of the law." [3] Such customs are enforced by social disapproval of any violation.

Christ has freed us from the tyranny of men's external standards of righteousness, and has put within us His standard of righteousness through the work of the Holy Spirit.

Paul's letter to the Galatian church denounces the Jews who were trying to add their customs as requirements for salvation. They were more comfortable with external codes of living than with faith in Christ, without which there is no salvation.

Today, we often find ourselves caught up in some legalistic custom we believe is necessary to our salvation. Some churches depend on a certain form of dress or religious rite which is performed regularly to ensure their righteousness. Entire religious systems have been developed around external rituals that in effect deny the sacrifice of Jesus. However, to place our trust in these religious customs negates the power of Christ's sacrifice on Calvary to effect our salvation (Gal. 2:21). Unless we place our trust in the death and resurrection of Christ for our salvation, and that of the world, we have no hope of being saved.

The power of that salvation will be nullified if we add anything to it. Wherever the Church has inadvertently included demands of custom as criteria for the Christ-life, it must repent and return to complete faith in the work of Calvary.

The Holy Spirit is faithful to speak truth to us as we open our hearts to hear Him. He was sent to guide us into all truth (John 16:13). We need not fear or despair that we will not know how to be delivered from our wrong thinking. As we listen to the Holy Spirit, and allow Him to convict and cleanse us, we will be prepared to be a part of the great revival that is coming.

The next move of God will not be like the charismatic renewal we have known in the past years. It will restore to the Church many things that the charismatic renewal did not restore. Yet we need to be grateful for the things that renewal brought, as we allow the Holy Spirit to teach us what is yet to come.

Part Three

The Charismatic Renewal
and the Next Move of God

Nine

THE CHARISMATIC RENEWAL
Blessings Restored

Throughout Church history there have been great visitations of the Holy Spirit that have restored wonderful truths to the Church, changed thousands of lives and often spawned new denominations. These supernatural visitations are seasons when God reveals Himself to people with hungry hearts and establishes them in the realities of redemptive truths. As the Church learns to walk in new realms of truth, the Holy Spirit enlarges her capacity to receive greater revelation of God. Thus once again He visits His people, bringing still new revelation of Himself.

Our generation received an outpouring of the Holy Spirit

that swept through many denominations, baptizing thousands of believers in the Holy Spirit. Some people have called this visitation from God the charismatic movement. However, it was not a move of God — it was a renewal. No significant new truth was restored to the Church during the charismatic renewal as in other historical moves of God. However, truths already present in the Church, such as the baptism of the Holy Spirit, were more firmly established across wider lines of religious thought, which helped to remove denominational barriers for many Christians.

Now, thirty years after the charismatic renewal began, some are inclined to speak lightly of that visitation of God, and others are even unkind in their attitudes toward it. They point to some negative results they have seen and, instead of evaluating it fairly, denounce it entirely. Though the charismatic renewal did sweep up some debris, as is typical of any wave of God, its effect on the Church was very positive. It brought blessings to the Church that were badly needed.

When a river floods its banks and the waters rush out of control, debris is carried along and washed up on dry ground. Whatever is situated in the middle of the river will experience the exhilaration of being swept along by the power of the flood. But whatever sloshes along in the muck and mire along the edge will end up with mud all over it.

So it is when God visits His people in a way that overwhelms our finite minds — we may not always interpret accurately everything an omnipotent God does. Though we do not understand completely, we may choose to enjoy the sweeping flood of God's presence by staying in the middle of the flowing waters. Or we may choose to concentrate on the debris by becoming critical of the work of God. Every time there has been a visitation of God throughout Church history, there also has been some controversial debris surrounding the work of God. The charismatic renewal was no exception.

When God showed the prophet Ezekiel the healing waters of revival (see Ezekiel 47), he saw waters ankle deep, knee deep, waters to the loins and waters to swim in. The good swimmer enjoys the deep water and is not concerned with the debris the waters might be sweeping up along the bank. So it is that Christians who choose to seek the deeper things of God will have a different perspective from those who are easily contented close to shore.

Those who enjoyed the waters of the charismatic renewal received great benefit from the good things it brought to their lives and to the Church.

The charismatic renewal was a true visitation of God and came in the timing of God. Thousands were swept into the fullness of the baptism of the Holy Spirit. I was brought in as a Methodist professor and minister along with many other denominational people. I thank God for His visitation during those years of renewal that established the Church in important truths. The Church would not have been ready for the coming next move of God had we not experienced the waters of the charismatic renewal.

There were several areas of truth that were strengthened in the Church during the years of the charismatic renewal.

Recognition of Spiritual Gifts

Before the charismatic renewal, many denominations, and even some Pentecostal churches, had "muzzled" the mouth of the Holy Spirit, not allowing Him to manifest the gifts of the Spirit in the Church. Some churches who professed to be Spirit-filled had relegated the moving of the Spirit to the basement. Not wanting to offend anyone during their liturgical Sunday morning services, they allowed the manifestation of the gifts of tongues or prophecy to be given only in a Wednesday night service in the basement when nobody but the "family" was present. Thus, in essence they were telling the Holy Ghost: "You can't do anything when we have visitors. Wait 'til nobody but us is here."

Since the charismatic renewal there has been a greater recognition of spiritual gifts in the Church. Even some denominations that have not accepted the gift of tongues are inviting Spirit-filled ministers to teach their congregations about spiritual gifts. As these sincere Christians open their hearts to the working of the Holy Spirit, He may slip in on them — as He did on me — the gift of tongues, also.

The Holy Spirit didn't ask my opinion on tongues. He just baptized me. I found myself speaking in tongues. Then He declared, as Peter declared on the day of Pentecost, "This is that which was spoken by the prophet Joel..."(Acts 2:16).

The day God baptized me in His Holy Spirit with the evidence of speaking in other tongues, He also healed me from a genetic bone disease which the doctors believed to be life-threatening. I did not ask for the baptism in the Holy Spirit because I thought I already had it. My theological viewpoint caused me to believe that speaking in tongues was for weak-minded people or emotional people. I thought I was too intelligent for such an experience. Frankly, I was too dumb.

So the Lord arranged desperate circumstances that made me cry out to Him. He knew my heart wanted Him, even though my head didn't understand His ways. He baptized me in the Holy Spirit and I spoke in other tongues even though I hadn't believed in it with my head.

From that experience I realized how little I knew of God's ways. The Holy Spirit became my faithful Teacher. He began to teach me the Word of God by revelation, and He has not stopped to this day. I am one of many sincere denominational believers who received a fullness of the Spirit during the charismatic renewal. I thank God that He overruled our theology and brought us to the scriptural recognition of spiritual gifts.

Faith

It is unfortunate that some charismatic teachers have swung the pendulum of faith too far, teaching a hyper-faith doctrine. But the charismatic renewal brought a desperately needed, new dimension of faith to the Church. Many Christians had a passive faith. They thought God *could*, but didn't believe He *would* move through His Spirit in today's world.

Many Christians did not believe that God still uses signs and wonders. They interpreted Paul's statement, "when that which is perfect is come, then that which is in part shall be done away" (1 Cor. 13:10), to mean that because the Word of God had come, the gifts of the Spirit were no longer necessary. The message of faith came to adjust our incorrect doctrine.

True faith is not given simply to bring us to personal salvation. Faith enables us to understand the eternal plan of God for the Church. That plan will be fulfilled sovereignly, as He has determined, to bring many sons to glory. True faith will be required to bring the purposes of God to pass in the earth.

Hebrews 11, the great faith "hall of fame," bears record that those individuals who dare to believe the promises of God receive His blessings and are able to accomplish great things in His name (see Hebrews 11).

Much erroneous doctrine concerning faith and unbelief was cleansed from the Church during the charismatic renewal as people began to believe God for miracles — and received them.

Misplaced Faith

Unfortunately, carnal Christians valued and desired temporal blessings more than eternal ones. The demand of many for material blessings led to what has been called the "prosperity doctrine." I do believe in prosperity, but I can't imagine having the audacity to demand that the almighty, omnipotent, omniscient, omnipresent, sovereign, infinite God do something to satisfy my desire for material things. Be careful to balance the message of faith with the sovereign will of God for His people. God cannot be treated as a Santa Claus. Though He has promised to give material blessings to His children, He expects us to use our faith on a higher plane that will help to effect His eternal purposes in the earth.

The charismatic renewal helped the Church renew its faith to believe God for miracles and to walk in the promises of the Word of God. Through it our vision has been lifted to expect to receive good things from our God according to His will. God is a good God — not a hard taskmaster. That reality was strengthened in the Church through the renewal of our faith.

Authority

The charismatic renewal also brought a realization of the authority of the believer. Some Christians did not even know they had power over the devil. The Spirit of God began to reveal the truth that "greater is he that is in you than he that is in the world" (1 John 4:4). Jesus told us, "In the world ye shall have tribulation." But He continued by saying: "Be of good cheer, I have overcome the world" (John 16:33). Paul taught us to be overcomers in Christ (Rom. 12:21).

Authority in Church Government

The lines of proper authority in the leadership of the Church was established during the charismatic renewal as well. Unfortunately, some debris was also swept up with the truth about spiritual authority as it became mixed with the carnal desire to rule, causing much grief to the Church.

Christ's authority may be defined as the power of attorney that enables one to do legal business for another in their absence (Luke 4:18). It is understood that the one to whom power of attorney has been given will follow the explicit instructions of the one who delegated that authority. In this sense, Jesus exercised His Father's power of attorney perfectly while He lived on the earth. Jesus declared: "The Son can do nothing of Himself, unless it is something He sees the Father doing; for whatever the Father does, these things the son also does in like manner (John 5:19b, NAS).

Church leaders need to exhibit the same integrity of heart and motivation in order to fulfill God's purpose for His authority in the Church. As we allow Christ to be the Head of His Church, walking humbly as His servants, we can know the true blessing of divine authority in the Church.

It is important to remember that Jesus gave His disciples authority over demons and diseases — not over one another (Luke 9:1). He told them not to lord it over each other as the gentiles did, but to become servants of all (Mark 10:42-44). The Holy Spirit wants to establish true biblical authority in Church government.

During the charismatic renewal, those who misunderstood divine authority confused it with their own carnal desire to rule. They caused much grief to sincere Christians who were willing to be led. Yet, in spite of the debris this misunderstanding caused, this truth about the authority of God needed to be restored in the Church.

An absence of true authority makes us vulnerable to the attacks of the enemy. As our understanding about God's authority is strengthened and we are cleansed from our carnal desire to rule, the Church will march triumphantly against all its external or internal foes. God's guidelines for authority protect believers and build a strong Church in the earth. We will see a healthy Church emerge as we follow them carefully.

The Joy of Giving

The fresh revelation about giving to the Lord was one of the greatest blessings of the charismatic renewal. God has a generous, giving nature. God is love. Because of His nature "He gave his only begotten Son, that whosoever believeth in him should not perish, but have everlasting life" (John 3:16). The entire Godhead is involved in this lavish giving. The

Father gave His best — His only Son — to redeem us. Jesus suffered crucifixion willingly that our relationship with Him might be restored. And the Holy Ghost is giving Himself wholly to reveal Jesus to us.

As children of God, we must experience and demonstrate this "family spirit" of divine love to the world. God's love impelled Him to give. If we love God, we will be impelled to give our best to God joyfully.

For many people, the joy of giving was a spontaneous response to the charismatic renewal as we suddenly realized we could invest in so many ways in an eternal kingdom — the kingdom of God.

Peter's Question

Peter asked the Lord, "Behold, we have forsaken all, and followed thee; what shall we have therefore?" (Matt. 19:27b). Some may criticize Peter for asking such a question. It may sound too much like: "What do we get out of this?"

I am thankful that Peter asked the question. Jesus' answer reveals the joy of giving and receiving in the kingdom of God: "Every one that hath forsaken houses, or brethren, or sisters, or father, or mother, or wife, or children, or lands, for my name's sake, shall receive an hundredfold, and shall inherit everlasting life" (Matt. 19:29b). What a tremendous promise! Our generous God has declared that whatever we give into His kingdom will be returned a hundredfold.

Have you ever tried to fold a sheet of paper a hundred times? A hundredfold is not 100 percent — it is much greater. While pastoring in Plano, Texas, several years ago (before the age of computers), I asked Texas Instruments to calculate a hundredfold. They sent back the message that they had exhausted their largest calculator at fifty-one fold! A hundredfold increase is an astronomical figure — beyond our ability to imagine. Yet Jesus promised a hundredfold to those who would leave all and follow Him.

According to Jesus' promise, whatever you invest — your time, talents, trusted possessions or anything else — He will give back to you a hundredfold. Understanding this principle, it wasn't any surprise to me when my Father told me recently that I was not going to die. I know, of course, that my physical body will be buried one day. But I will live on through the lives of people in whom I have invested — preaching to them and seeing them transformed by the power of God. In turn, they will preach to others who will be redeemed for eternity as well.

The precious truths God has revealed to me will also be preserved through books and tapes for the body of Christ to enjoy. The multiplication of my time, talent, testimony and gifts will continue, and I will enjoy the fruit of its return throughout all eternity.

Recognition of the Church

The charismatic renewal also brought a recognition of the body of Christ — the Church — as it is described in the New Testament. We have not always had a clear understanding of God's intent for the Church. Too often we have viewed it as a social organization with certain religious practices and delegated responsibilities to its constituents. That is not the biblical description of the Church.

A Body

According to the Scriptures, the Church is a living organism of which Christ is the Head (Eph. 4:15). Paul the apostle declared that the Church is a body, "fitly joined together and compacted by that which every joint supplieth, according to the effectual working in the measure of every part" (Eph. 4:16).

Paul told the Corinthians that we are all "baptized into one body" (1 Cor. 12:13). Then he continued by saying, "For the body is not one member, but many" (vs. 14). Each member, though different from the others, is necessary and important to the body.

Paul did not use the body as an analogy of the Church, as some have taught, for he plainly declares: "Now ye *are* the body of Christ, and members in particular" (1 Cor. 12:27, italics added). An analogy shows a likeness or similarity to something described. However, Paul declares that in reality we *are* the body of Christ — the Church. This mystery of the Church being the body of Christ is being revealed more clearly in these days.

Pastor Sue Curran, conference speaker, teacher and popular author, has observed the blessing of the true Church:

> Through the Church, the triune Godhead receives distinctive blessings from believers. The Holy Spirit is given a temple to live in, Jesus is given a body, and the Father is given a family to love.[1]

This understanding of the Church as the body of Christ

is different from the concept of a church as a loose-knit group of people who meet together once or twice a week for "worship."

The Body Functioning

It takes all of us to make up the body of Christ. In teaching this reality, Paul the apostle declared that we have some uncomely parts that are just as necessary as the more comely ones. Without them the body dies. As members of Jesus' body, we are responsible to supply what other brothers and sisters need. We do not live for ourselves, nor are we to be secret disciples. You contribute to my life in God and I contribute to yours.

Perhaps you do not recognize your contribution to the Church. You may consider yourself simply an "attender." But your faith, prayers and love can make a valuable contribution to the spiritual life of others as you give what you have. Knowing that you belong and are needed brings health to your psyche and fulfillment to your life.

One morning as I walked through the sanctuary before the Sunday morning service, I felt discouraged. I prayed, "Jesus, please put Your arms around me this morning. Please hold me. I just want to feel loved. I need someone to hold me."

When the service started, the love of God flowed freely among the people, and the Holy Spirit began to melt hearts. One by one, people moved around, hugging one another and praying together. The children and teenagers ran to the platform to hug me, and many adults followed to show their love. Refreshed in my spirit, I thought, Isn't this wonderful?

After a while I heard my Father say to me, "How do you like the love I sent you?" The expressed love of the body of Christ had encouraged my heart and met my need to feel loved that morning.

Every Joint Supplies

Terry Clark, a young man in my church, heard me speak one Sunday morning about "every joint supplying" in the body of Christ. He went home for dinner after the service, and then lay down to take a nap. That evening, the service was already in progress when this tall young man ran into the church. Excitedly, he said, "I am sorry I am late; I overslept. I have come to be a joint to supply." If everyone realized their responsibility to be a "joint supplier" to the body of Christ, they would be more willing to give joyfully of what they have. And in that joy of giving, they would find themselves receiving as well.

Temporal Blessings

The charismatic renewal prepared the Church in many ways to receive what God has purposed to give her in His next visitation. The Church does not yet have all she needs to become the glorious Church God intends. For that to happen, we must look to the next move of God.

Many of the blessings of the charismatic renewal, though necessary, are temporal. Though these temporal blessings prepare us for the next move of God, they won't be needed when we get to heaven. We won't need faith, for our faith will become sight as we see Him face to face. There will be no enemies to overcome. Nor will the gifts of the Spirit be necessary for the edifying of the Church. Having acknowledged these blessings for the good they have brought, the Church is in need of something greater than these temporal blessings to fulfill her destiny.

The Church developed charisma during the charismatic renewal, but she did not develop character. The mature Church described by Paul in his christological epistles has not yet emerged. In fact, the Church became self-centered even in the midst of renewal. Seeking for personal satisfaction in spiritual gifts, ministries and material possessions, many lost sight of valuable qualities that would prepare them to meet the Father.

God has the Church hidden in various "caves" of circumstance to cleanse her from selfishness and wrong motivations. He wants her attention to be focused on Jesus and what He is doing. With that change of focus we will be ready to receive everything the next move of God will bring. And we will understand that the temporal blessings derived from the charismatic renewal were mere stepping stones. With the next move of God, these temporal blessings will fade away in the revelation of the eternal.

Part Four

The New Blessing
of the Next Move of God

What can we expect to happen in the believer's life, and in the Church, in the next move of God?

The Scriptures reveal God's intent for the Church in the next move of God. They declare plainly what He will do in these last days. The following chapters will make clear the revelation of God's wonderful plan of revival for His people. Allow your faith to rise in anticipation of becoming a partaker of the great blessings that are coming.

> For since the beginning of the world men have
> not heard, nor perceived by the ear, neither hath
> the eye seen, O God, beside thee, what he hath
> prepared for him that waiteth for him (Is. 64:4).

The revelation that awaits us is so wonderful that none of us will be able to say, "I knew this was coming." We cannot imagine what the great love of God has in store for those who wait for Him.

Ten

HOLINESS

The Character of God

One of the more obvious blessings God will bring to the Church in the next move of God is holiness. Both the Old and New Testaments are filled with admonitions to holiness. Our "cave" experiences will bring us to a walk of holiness that we have never known — or even desired — before now. The Scriptures declare that the purpose for God's chastening upon our lives is that we might be "partakers of his holiness" (Heb. 12:10).

Holiness is not who *we* are; it is who *God* is. Holiness is the character of God. The name of the third Person of the Godhead — Holy Spirit — reveals that God's nature is holiness. The holiness of God is a wonderful study, its thread running throughout the Bible from beginning to end.

When the Scriptures help us to peer into heaven, we hear the cherubim crying, "Holy, holy, holy" (Is. 6:3). Perhaps they cry "holy" once for the Father, once for the Son and once for the Holy Spirit. It will be glorious when they can add a fourth "holy" for the Church — the bride of Christ.

God's Plan for Holiness

When God made mankind He did not give us *eternal* life; He gave us *immortal* life. Immortality simply means we are destined to live somewhere forever. Where we live will be our choice. In order to live forever with God, we have to choose to receive eternal life.

God chose to make man in His own image. However, being made in God's image did not automatically give man God's character, His holiness. Image was God's choice; character was to be mankind's choice. Adam and Eve would have attained holiness of character if they had chosen to obey God in their testings.

God wanted to receive love from mankind. He desired to reproduce Himself in mankind. However, by definition, love is not a response that can be coerced or forced; it is a result of man's free choice. God wanted mankind to respond to His love by choosing to obey Him and walk in fellowship with Him. In that way, the character of God would be formed in man through the process of his right choices.

God offered Adam and his wife the choice of eternal life with Him and placed the tree of life in the garden. They could choose to eat of that tree. He also placed the tree of the knowledge of good and evil in the garden, and told them not to eat of that tree. If they ate of it they would die. It was the only tree they were not to eat (Gen. 2:16-17).

But the serpent deceived Eve, and both Adam and Eve ate of the forbidden tree. Their choice to disobey the command of God caused death to come, not only to them, but to all mankind. In making their choice to disobey God, they severed their relationship with Him, forfeiting eternal life.

In His high priestly prayer (John 17), Jesus defined eternal life for us.

> And this is life eternal, that they might know
> thee the only true God, and Jesus Christ, whom
> thou hast sent (John 17:3).

Enjoying relationship with God is the essence of eternal life. By disobedience, Adam and Eve died to their relationship with God, thus failing to gain eternal life. Instead of allowing His character to be developed in them through obedience to His Word, they condemned all of mankind to disobedience.

Our Plight

The world has been eating from the tree of the knowledge of good and evil ever since Adam and Eve's fateful choice. From that tree we get all our pagan philosophies: humanism, atheism, skepticism, New Age and others. Our world is now partaking of that tree more than ever. We partake of that tree almost every time we turn the TV on; public schools feed our children a steady diet of it; and the world's governments face overwhelming problems without remedy because of the fruit of that tree.

God's Remedy

God was not surprised by mankind's treason in the garden of Eden. From before the foundation of the world, God had initiated His plan of redemption to redeem mankind from his own destructive choices. In the fullness of time, God replanted the tree of life — on the hill of Golgotha — through Jesus' ultimate sacrifice on the cross. Because of that sacrifice, mankind can now choose to receive eternal life, this time by accepting the sacrifice of Christ's blood on the cross.

In mercy, God gave the law of Moses to those who lived before Christ so that by submitting to prescribed sacrificial rituals they could have the hope of eternal life. They looked forward to Christ's perfect sacrifice on the cross; we look back to it. It is the only source of eternal life.

He that hath the Son hath life; and he that hath not the Son of God hath not life (1 John 5:12).

To choose Christ is to choose eternal life. To not choose Christ is to forfeit eternal life. The wonderful miracle of salvation happens as we choose to accept Christ as our Savior. He places an "incorruptible seed" of life in our spirit, and we become alive to God (1 Pet. 1:23). When that happens, not only will we live forever in immortality, but we have made our choice to receive the gift of eternal life.

The Choice of Transformation

It was a powerful revelation when I learned that through the God-given power of choice, I could begin to develop His character after salvation. As we choose to obey the Word of God, our minds are transformed to think the way God thinks. By choosing to walk in obedience, responding correctly to life's trials, we allow God to develop His holiness in us.

God will never force His character on us. He waits for us to choose to exchange self-life for His divine nature. That choice must be made, not once, but in every situation of life where we find our will or nature to be contrary to His. As we learn to yield to the will of God, we can rest in Him, knowing that we cannot produce holiness in ourselves. Holiness is God's character produced in us by the Holy Spirit as a result of our yielding to His working in our lives.

The trees in the garden of Eden were put there to provide for and test mankind. Adam and Eve could have had not only God's image, but His character as well. The choice was theirs.

In Christ, we can choose to receive God's character. We will be going "home" with the character of the last Adam — Christ — formed in us. We will have the spirit of the family, God's family traits of love, holiness and integrity, so that we won't be "misfits" in the Father's house.

Sanctification

The Scriptures declare: "For this is the will of God, even your sanctification" (1 Thess. 4:3a). Sanctification is the biblical term for the process of becoming holy. Sanctification is not what we do to make ourselves holy, as some have taught. Though it is true that we must cooperate with the Holy Spirit, sanctification is primarily His working in us through the cross.

Holiness is not an external code of living. Holiness is not what clothes or jewelry we wear. Because of a faulty definition of holiness, I spent seventeen years trying to make the part of me look holy that they are going to put in the cemetery — not even wearing a simple gold wedding band. Unfortunately, my external code of holiness did not result in my sanctification. Instead, I lived in bondage and legalism, becoming critical and judgmental of others who did not dress as I did.

A Command

Holiness is a command of God for all believers. Peter admonished believers to "be holy yourselves also in all your behavior; because it is written, You shall be holy, for I am holy" (1 Pet. 1:15-16, NAS). Throughout the Bible holiness is given as a command, not an option. Holiness will continue to be the theme of eternity. "Holiness unto the Lord" is on the priest's crown and engraved on his garments (see Exodus 28). That phrase will even be inscribed on the pots and pans in the millennium (Zech. 14:20). Such emphasis on holiness means we are going to have to become holy to be a part of God's kingdom.

Only to the degree that we die to self can we develop the character of God within our lives. We must renounce the humanistic doctrine that man is basically good. We are sinners — lost, undone, aliens to God. Improving our self-image will not eradicate our sin nature.

God's character will become the character of believers. He *will* have a glorious Church without spot or wrinkle. We are going home in His holiness. When Lucifer fell from heaven God also kicked out rebellion, selfishness and independence. He is not going to allow it to enter again. Holiness is not an option; it is a command.

Two Elements of Sanctification

There are two primary elements of sanctification: the Holy Spirit's work; and my cooperation with Him. Sanctification sets the believer apart by God for His use. We cannot be set apart until we are willing to come apart from other pursuits. We have to come out of worldly lifestyles, forsake other interests and be committed to do His will in order to be set apart.

A second aspect of sanctification is the resultant work by the power of the Spirit of God that literally changes our lives — producing true holiness. The work of sanctification takes us to the cross again and again. It exposes our carnal nature and makes us cry out to be delivered. We realize that we are powerless to deliver ourselves. But as we submit to the testings and dealings of God, we find wonderful deliverance from our self-life and a continual infilling with Himself.

Conquering "Self"

As long as we love our self-life, we will keep it. We must hate our self-life in order to be delivered from it. When certain Greek men came to see Jesus, He told them: "Except a corn [kernel] of wheat fall into the ground and die, it abideth alone: but if it die, it bringeth forth much fruit" (John 12:24). In this picture of the seed shedding its hard outer shell in death so that new life could come forth, Jesus was showing them the necessity of hating their self-life.

There is a holy cry that is birthed by the Spirit of God in our spirit against everything that is unclean and destructive to body, soul and spirit. If that holy hatred for sin and self does not come, we will never be cleansed; and the life of Christ will not be seen in us.

Isaiah voiced that cry before the throne of God. As he was given a vision of God in His holiness, he recognized his own uncleanness and cried out:

> Woe is me, for I am undone; because I am a man
> of unclean lips, and I dwell in the midst of a peo-
> ple of unclean lips: for mine eyes have seen the
> King, the Lord of hosts (Is. 6:5).

Isaiah had to see the holiness of God before he could see his own unclean condition. Then as a coal from the altar was placed on his lips by one of the seraphim, he was cleansed.

I once heard a minister declare that he didn't know the Lord. When I heard him say that, I sat in my self-righteousness and became angry with him. *Why was he in the pulpit preaching if he did not know Jesus? What was he saying?* I was still stewing in my anger when I went to bed that night.

But the Holy Ghost didn't let me sleep. He revealed my own vile self-life. In that awful revelation, I understood what the minister meant when he confessed he didn't know God. He meant that his knowledge of God was very limited in comparison to the reality of who God is. He was declaring, as Paul did, "I count all things but loss for the excellency of the knowledge of Christ Jesus my Lord" (Phil. 3:8a).

Until we see our selfishness, "unlove" and pride as God sees it, we will not experience a godly hatred for it. But when we do, we will cry with Isaiah: "Woe is me" (Is. 6:5). We will wait for the cleansing coal from the altar to purge our iniquity. We will not see our need for sanctification if we use ourselves or others as the standard of holiness. But when we behold God in His righteousness we see, in contrast, our lack of holiness — and can then be changed.

Before I go to my Father I will be changed into His image by His grace. By making right choices I can have His character and His holiness. The tree of life — the Christ-life — that is planted within me transforms me into His character as I yield to Him continually. Paul understood this, and wrote: "Christ in you, the hope of glory" (Col. 1:27). The cleansing work of the Holy Spirit releases the life of Christ in us, and as we yield to Him we realize true holiness in our lives and in our churches.

Eleven

HOLINESS REALIZED
God's Character in the Church

E very child of God who sincerely desires to grow in the Lord will come to that place of "holy desperation" where our soul cries out with the psalmist, "Wash me throughly from mine iniquity, and cleanse me from my sin" (Ps. 51:2).

There are those who are so calloused that they have no sense of guilt and can sin easily. They are no longer sensitive to the sweet convictions of the Holy Spirit! Such souls may drift farther and farther away from the Lord until a devastating, drastic test snaps them out of their apathy and brings them back to God. But the earnest, honest Christian finds no rest or peace until he bows low at the feet of his Lord in open and full confession, seeking forgiveness and cleansing for the stain upon his soul.

Basis for Cleansing

If we confess our sins, he is faithful and just to forgive us our sins, and to cleanse us from all unrighteousness (1 John 1:9).

That verse is the basis for our cleansing from the stain of sin. God can never forgive hidden sin. Tears, weeping or remorse will never bring forgiveness. Only wholehearted confession can bring forgiveness, restore fellowship with God and bring His blessings into our lives.

In the Greek, *confession* is a poignant word that means "to speak the same thing; to say back to God what His Holy Spirit says to us."[1] When the Holy Spirit convicts us of a mean spirit toward another, it is hypocritical to say, "Yes, Lord, I do lack love for that person." When the Holy Spirit reveals the abomination of our pride, it is quite beside the point to say, "Yeah, Lord, I need a little more humility." God will not receive such confessions.

True Confession

How precious was the confession of God's servant David! After David sent Uriah to the front and gave the command for all others to withdraw so that Uriah would be killed, God spoke to him through the prophet Nathan: "Thou hast killed Uriah the Hittite with the sword, and hast taken his wife to be thy wife" (2 Sam. 12:9). Although David did not throw the spear that killed Uriah, he plotted Uriah's death, and God said: "Thou hast slain him." God laid the guilt right at David's feet.

David cried, "Deliver me from bloodguiltiness, O God, thou God of my salvation" (Ps. 51:14). In this mighty outpouring of his heart David continued: "Purge me with hyssop, and I shall be clean: wash me, and I shall be whiter than snow" (vs. 7).

Hyssop was a little shrub that was used to apply the blood and water of purification. Bunches of hyssop were used to sprinkle blood on the doorposts in Egypt (Ex. 12:22) and to purify the leper (Lev. 14:4-6). David's confession was real. He was saying back to God what God said to him concerning his sin.

Confessing Only "Sin"

It is our sin that we are to confess. God does not forgive mistakes; He either overlooks them or corrects us for them. God does not forgive doctrinal error — He corrects it. God does not forgive weaknesses; He strengthens us so as to deliver us from them. God forgives sin. When we come to Him for forgiveness, we come with a full consciousness of sin, or we come not at all.

Sin Defined

True, the word *sin* has gone out of vogue in modernistic theology and psychology. It is now defined by such high-sounding and euphemistic phrases as human weakness, negative thinking, maladjustment or emotional disturbance.

It is even rationalized as "upset nerves." But God calls sin, *sin,* and He forgives only sin!

What, indeed, is sin? We need to come to a renewed and fresh revelation of all that constitutes sin. Sin is the transgression of the law, but it is more. Generally speaking, sin is everything contrary to the nature and will of God. Sin is the opposite of holiness. It is all unrighteousness, all that is ungodly. It is all that is opposed to God or independent from God.

According to the Scriptures, there are sins of commission and sins of omission. There are the sins of the self-life and sins of the spirit. There is manifest sin; and there is hidden, secret sin. One can sin in thought, word and deed.

Make no mistake about it — God hates all sin. Being a holy God, He could not do otherwise. But because He is a God of love, He loves the sinner. This goodness of God leads us to repentance (Rom. 2:4).

Sin acts as a disease to the soul in the same way that cancer does to the body. It disintegrates personality, affects bodily health adversely, darkens one's mind and sears the conscience. Furthermore, it always breaks, or makes impossible, one's fellowship with his Maker. It causes untold misery in human relationships. Sin is the cause of all war. It fills our jails, our prisons and our state hospitals.

We tend to rank sin in our church teachings, thinking that some sins are more wicked than others. We say murder or adultery are gross sins. We may determine others to be minor — such as the proverbial white lie. God does not categorize sin by degrees. Sin is sin if it violates God's law. Anxiety is sin. Unbelief is sin. Selfishness is sin. Worldliness is sin. In these days, above all else God's people need an acute sense of sin.

Anything that separates me from God, or from my brother in Christ, is sin.

The Scriptures teach only one way to deal with sin: confession. We must always confess our sins to God! And we must confess them to the people against whom we committed the sins. It is important to realize that we cannot get right with God if we do not make things right with men (Matt. 18:15-17, 35).

When we do go to another to be reconciled, we are to confess only our fault. It matters not what fault the other may have had; we commit that to the Lord and pray for that person. God does not ask us to confess another's sin; He asks that we confess our sin.

Let us suppose that we have uttered some unkind remark or some untruth about a person to a third party. To whom do we confess? We go to the one to whom the remark was made; and, if we have any reason to believe that the one spoken about knows of what we said, then we are to go to him also. I believe that if the one wronged does not know of our hurtful remarks about him, then we should hold our peace lest we create further offense.

But having confessed our sin to both God and man, can we be sure that God will always forgive our sins? Yes, hallelujah! We have His promise that He will forgive us:

> If we confess our sins, he is faithful and just to forgive us our sins, and to cleanse us from all unrighteousness (1 John 1:9).

God is both faithful and just to forgive our sin, and to cleanse every stain.

God's outraged holiness against sin has been fully satisfied at Calvary. His wrath is not as man's wrath — it is the awful reaction of His holy nature against sin. The wrath of God has had full expression. When Jesus hung on Calvary's cross, the full force of God's outraged holiness found expression as He turned His face away from His own Son, who was made sin for us, that we might be made the righteousness of God in Him (2 Cor. 5:21). Because God's holiness has been vindicated, He can now be "just" in forgiving sinful man.

Oh, with what utter confidence then can we come to God with our sins! How utterly sure we can be of His forgiveness when we confess our sins sincerely. Our sins have already been dealt with, God's holiness has been vindicated, and it is possible for Him to forgive us. What joy fills the soul of him who comes to God in full contrition of heart and brokenness of spirit to confess his sins! What rest and peace is his who *knows* that God has forgiven his sin. The stain of it is wiped out forever, and God remembers it against him no more! What a sense of relief is his whose burden of sin is gone! How quickly then our fellowship with God is restored!

Cleansing From the Power of Sin

Confession deals only with sins committed and their stain upon the soul. What about the power of sin that manifests itself in thought, word or deed? Many of God's children sin and confess their sins over and over again because they do not know the way of true deliverance from the power of sin. They live an up-and-down existence of continual sin and confession.

There is a way to live in continual victory over sin. God wants to bring us into a highway of holiness. He made full provision for breaking the *power* of sin, just as He made provision for cleansing the *stain* of sin.

Walking in the Light

How do we come onto God's highway of holiness so we need not confess the same sins all the time? How can we live in full and unbroken fellowship with God? The Bible declares:

> If we walk in the light, as he is in the light, we
> have fellowship one with another, and the blood
> of Jesus Christ his Son cleanseth us from all sin
> (1 John 1:7).

God's cleansing from the power of sin is conditional — we must walk in the light. He is that light. His light comes into our souls with revelation from heaven. It is the divine light we receive by being joined to the Lord as a branch to the vine, letting His life become our life. We cannot, in ourselves, overcome the power of sin anymore than we could cleanse away the stain of committed sins. But there is provision for both in Christ.

It would be wonderful if someone could break the power of sin for us by laying hands on us and praying for us. But deliverance from the power of sin does not come that way. Sin's power is broken as we daily walk in the light. Sin's power is conquered as we daily take the cross presented to us in the power of the crucified Christ. The blood of Christ keeps cleansing us from the power of sin as we keep walking in the light.

If we fail or refuse to walk in the light, Satan can again put us under his malicious power. But as we walk in the light, the blood of Jesus Christ remains efficacious to breaking Satan's power over us forever. As we call upon the mighty power of Christ when Satan comes to tempt us, we find that every place of former defeat becomes a place of triumph.

It is one thing to experience the glory and the relief that comes from a deep sense of forgiven sins, but it is quite another thing to experience that greater glory and release that comes because the power of sin is broken. We may momentarily stumble as we walk the highway of God's holiness, yet if our face is steadfastly set toward God, we shall rest upon His everlasting arms. A full confession will bring quick recovery, and we can resume our pilgrimage God-ward.

True holiness characterizes God's people. As the Holy Spirit is poured out in revival we are going to know His convicting and cleansing power. It will bring momentary pain. But we will know great release and victory as His cleansing power breaks our bondage to sin. What joy is in store for the people who will follow their God in holiness! Surely it will be joy unspeakable and full of glory!

Twelve

REVIVAL THROUGH GLADNESS

Holy Ghost Joy

There is a wonderful supernatural joy spreading throughout the Church around the world today. It is both a supernatural sign and an impartation from the Lord. The Scriptures, both Old and New Testaments, are full of the promise of joy for the people of God. Yet we have seen very little joy in the Church until this most recent outpouring. Perhaps this fact, more than any other, reflects the backslidden state of the Church that so needs to be revived.

The Scriptures declare: "Because you did not serve the Lord your God with joy and a glad heart, for the abundance of all things: therefore you shall serve your enemies" (Deut. 28:47-48, NAS). The children of Israel went into captivity

119

because they did not serve God joyfully. The people of God have submitted to many yokes of bondage simply because they did not cultivate a joyful heart in serving God. The two extremes of bondage — legalism and license — have crippled much of the Church today. Legalism is the inordinate regard for rules as a means of salvation. License is the opposite of legalism. It is a disregard for rules and the irresponsible use of freedom (see 1 Cor. 8:9).

God looks upon us with compassion. He wants to return and gather us from all the places where we have been scattered by our disobedience. He longs to turn our captivity so that we experience the reality of joy in our lives and churches (Deut. 30:1-3).

Jesus' Promise of Joy

To His disciples, Jesus declared the reason for teaching the truths of the kingdom:

> That my joy might remain in you, and that your joy might be full (John 15:11).

He intended for His followers to be full of joy. The Scriptures declare that God had anointed Jesus with the oil of gladness above His fellows (Heb. 1:9b). Joy filled Jesus as He lived on this earth. And joy was the deep motivation that empowered Jesus to go to the cross: "Who for the joy that was set before him endured the cross, despising the shame" (Heb. 12:2).

The Kingdom Is Joy

If we are not experiencing the joy of the Lord, we have not understood the good news of the gospel. The kingdom of God is defined as "righteousness, and peace, and joy in the Holy Ghost" (Rom. 14:17). If we do not experience the joy of the Lord, we have forfeited one third of the kingdom reality. Right relationship with Jesus will result in bringing joy to our lives.

The psalmist David understood that right relationship with God produced great joy. He wrote: "But let all those that put their trust in thee rejoice: let them ever shout for joy, because thou defendest them: let them also that love thy name be joyful in thee" (Ps. 5:11).

Rejoicing and shouting for joy are very energetic emotional responses to the presence of God. When we touch the kingdom of God we, like David, will respond joyfully to Him.

Joy Defined

Several Greek words can be translated "joy." The word *chara* denotes a sense of physical comfort and well-being. It is an inner gladness, a deep-seated pleasure, delight, relish, enjoyment.[1] The reality of joy brings great comfort and satisfaction to the human heart. Joy also brings a depth of assurance that ignites and overflows from a cheerful heart.[2]

The Holy Spirit produces that kind of joy in our lives as a fruit of the Spirit (Gal. 5:22). It is not a human emotion that can be attained through human effort. Joy is found only through relationship with God. It is an expression of godly emotion that springs from the inner being of one who is moved by love for God.

Another Greek word, *agalliasis,* signifies "exaltation, exuberant joy; an outward demonstration of joy or exaltation, as experienced in public worship" (see Acts 2:6).[3] David experienced that reality as he shouted for joy because of God's goodness (Ps. 42:4). Joy is more than an emotion; it is a vehicle for expressing what God is doing in the Spirit. It is not a mere display of human feelings, but a spiritual expression of divine happiness that comes as a result of God's wonderful intervention in our lives.

The joy of the Christian is not dependent on circumstances. It is not our environment, the people around us or the events we are going through that determine our joy or lack of it. The joy of the Holy Ghost causes us to live in trust even in the most trying circumstances. Human happiness looks at things on the earth and is affected by its conditions. Divine joy looks heaven-ward. It is unaffected by people, events or surrounding conditions because heaven's benefits are unchanging. As we learn to live in the kingdom of God, we will experience His righteousness, peace and joy. Our bondages will be broken and we will be released from our captivity to the enemy's purposes.

Release From Captivity

When the Lord turned again the captivity of Zion, we were like them that dream. Then was our mouth filled with laughter, and our tongue with singing (Ps. 126:1-2).

God will do the unusual and unexpected when He begins to revive His people. In some places where revival showers are beginning to break, we are seeing hundreds of people saved, brought into the Church, baptized in the Holy Spirit and healed.

One pastor whose church is in revival said his church had experienced more ministry in the past three months than in all its former years. That is only one example of the phenomenal ways God moves when He turns the captivity of His people.

Two Ways Joy Comes

Sovereign release from captivity is one way God uses to bring great joy to those who have been enslaved and separated from their homeland. The kingdom of Judah experienced this joy after they had been in captivity in Babylon for 70 years, continually dreaming of their homeland. Finally, Cyrus, the Persian king who conquered Babylon, unexpectedly declared the Jews free to return to Palestine (2 Chron. 36:22-23). Freedom broke in on them as a wild and beautiful dream. Their mouths were filled with laughter, and they were like those who dreamed (Ps. 126:1,2a).

Never before had a captive nation been released to return to its homeland. God had done it. Even the pagan nations around were astonished. They declared: "The Lord has done great things for them" (Ps. 126:2b). The Jews acknowledged they had done nothing to bring about this fortuitous turn of events. In gratitude for their sovereign deliverance, they echoed the cry of the heathen, "The Lord has done great things for us; whereof we are glad" (Ps. 126:3).

123

Sowing in Tears

When God comes sovereignly to destroy our bondages, it is a source of great joy. However, in the course of life, such events cannot occur continually. The psalmist recognized that. After rehearsing the joy of release from captivity, it is as though we can hear him heave a big sigh. Then he cries, "Turn again our captivity, O Lord, as the streams in the south. They that sow in tears shall reap in joy" (Ps. 126:4-5).

The psalmist is now praying for the remaining exiles in Babylon, for only a few of the exiled Jews had returned to their homeland in the first wave of freedom. He was asking the Lord to bring the rest of them home. His cry is sowing in tears. This second experience will also result ultimately in rejoicing. The psalmist understood that joy can also come as a result of sowing in tears. This source of joy is different from the sovereign intervention of God; it requires our obedience to the principle of sowing.

Jesus gave us the principle of sowing in His parable of the sower who planted seed faithfully in many kinds of soil. Some of the seed fell into places where it could not grow well. But others fell on good ground and brought forth fruit, some an hundredfold, some sixty and some thirtyfold (Matt. 13:3-9). Jesus explained to His disciples that the seed was the Word of God, and the ground was the hearts of people.

Nothing happens until the sower sows, though not all sowing brings good results. Our tears, in part, are the result of our unrewarded labor. Maybe we have shed tears over an unbelieving co-worker, one who demonstrated an Absalom spirit. Perhaps a neighbor we have been witnessing to for years still shows no receptivity. Maybe our ministry has not been well received and we have little to show for years of heart-breaking work. The process of sowing is often accompanied by tears.

Revival is good news for those faithful servants of God who have invested their time in people with little or no response. Many Christians have poured their lives into a ministry without seeing much fruitfulness. The psalmist declares a wonderful promise for those faithful servants who sow in tears, giving the precious seed of the Word to people who do not respond positively or wholeheartedly to the Lord. There is coming a day when the sower shall come again "with a shout of joy, bringing his sheaves with him" (Ps. 126:6b, NAS). The often agonizing labor of sowing will result in a joyful harvest.

That is a fact of life and a promise of God. Though we sow in tears for many years, facing difficulties, disappointments and even despair, we must keep sowing. If we give up too easily the process shuts down. The Holy Spirit within us is our source of power, but if we do not do our part to keep sowing, the principle fails and there will be no harvest. In the midst of tough times we need to trust God, knowing that the principle of sowing and reaping are in force. It is sowing, though it be done in tears, that is the source of deep, hard-won joy when the harvest is reaped.

A Revival of Joy

In the next move of God that is even now upon us, we see Him bringing a fresh anointing of joy to heal and empower His Church to go out into the harvest. It seems He is releasing us sovereignly from our captivity and bringing great joy to the Church. He is healing the wounds of the Church through this baptism of joy.

The Scriptures declare that a joyful heart is good medicine (Prov. 17:22). Medical science provides medicines to fight physical illness and painkillers to provide a temporary sense of well-being. But a heart made merry by God can cure us physically, spiritually, emotionally and mentally. As the Church is healed of her backsliding and wounds and filled with the joy of the Lord, she will be empowered to "go out with joy and be led forth with peace" (Is. 55:12). She will be equipped to go out to the harvest with the joy of the Lord as her strength (Neh. 8:10).

Manifestations of Joy

When Jesus said, "He that believeth on me, as the scripture hath said, out of his belly shall flow rivers of living water" (John 7:38), He was speaking of the Holy Spirit. The Spirit had not yet come to fill His people. As the Holy Spirit visits His people afresh, these rivers of life will bring joy and gladness, rejoicing and laughter.

The time of mourning is over, and God is restoring joy to His people. We cry with the psalmist: "Make us glad according to the days wherein thou hast afflicted us, and the years wherein we have seen evil" (Ps. 90:15). The end of our "cave" experiences will be the joyful celebration of a new anointing to walk in victory with our God.

However the Holy Spirit touches our emotions, the result will be spiritual refreshing, breaking of bondages and release of His divine life within us. Perhaps our natural reserve or cultural backgrounds make us fearful of entering into the joy of the Lord with abandon. Our part is simply to trust Him and yield to His moving, allowing Him to fill us with Himself.

Real or Counterfeit?

The fact of a counterfeit presupposes the reality of whatever is being counterfeited. There could be no counterfeit money, for example, without the real to copy. In the Spirit's present visitation of joy, the reality of an encounter with God must be experienced before real joy can manifest. Anything else will be counterfeit. However, the promises of God are sure to those who seek Him sincerely. God will not disappoint those who seek Him with an honest heart.

God is not limited in His methods. Sometimes God allows us to enjoy that which is out of the ordinary, as long as its precedent is scriptural. In this revival of joy that is spreading worldwide, we are hearing of people falling into trances. Even young children are being slain in the Spirit, experiencing visions and hearing God speak to them. God is visiting His people with a new anointing of joy and using phenomena which are extraordinary, yet biblical.

In both the Old and New Testaments there are recorded incidences of people falling into trances when they experienced a divine encounter with God. God caused a deep sleep to fall on Adam so that he could take a rib from him (Gen. 2:21). A deep sleep fell on Abraham when God came to covenant with him (Gen. 15:12). Daniel sank into a deep sleep when the angel of the Lord talked with him (Dan. 8:18). The apostle Paul fell into a trance when he was praying in the temple (Acts 22:17). Peter was resting on the roof one day when he fell into a trance and had an encounter with God (Acts 10:10).

There are other examples of people in the Scriptures who met God in an extraordinary way and received revelation from Him, such as John on the isle of Patmos.

The trance experiences accompanying this move of God are doing a deeper work in the believer than what occurred when people were slain in the Spirit during the charismatic renewal, though the manifestation is the same. In this present anointing, God is communing Spirit to spirit through the trance experience. He is arresting these believers in order to do a deep sovereign work in them that changes their lives.

Though His manifestation in the charismatic renewal was anointed, many believers did not seem to experience the deep healing and deliverance that people are giving testimony to now. These are "time outs" with God, during which He speaks to people, gives visions of heaven and works great deliverance in their lives. Many testify that in these moments with God He has done for them what counseling sessions could not do. The work that is done in His presence is eternal.

New Wine

In some churches, the Holy Spirit is pouring out a "new wine" anointing that makes people behave as though they were drunk. It is as on the day of Pentecost, when people looking on supposed the disciples were drunk. At a later time Paul admonished Christians: "And be not drunk with wine, wherein is excess; but be filled with the Spirit" (Eph. 5:18). It is significant that he links the state of drunkenness with being filled with the Spirit.

A minister that I know asked the Lord why people were getting drunk in the Spirit.

"I have to get My people drunk in My Spirit because they have been drunk on the world," the Lord responded. "Their minds have been polluted. They have fed their doubts, denying confidence in Me and My power. I have to get them so drunk that I can change their thoughts and their attitudes."

During revival the Holy Spirit comes with power. He has the freedom to move in supernatural ways to do supernatural works in believers. We do not need to fear the supernatural manifestations of the presence of God.

He does that which no man could do. When a believer comes from the presence of the Lord, healing and deliverance have taken place. Grief and sorrow are changed into joy. Coldness of heart is replaced by a fiery love for God.

My Baptism of Joy

The day after I was baptized in the Holy Spirit, a visible, small cloud came into my kitchen. I was a little Methodist woman who had never seen anything like that. Everywhere I went from the thirteenth day of April to the last day of September of 1959, that cloud went with me. It grew larger, blacker, more pregnant. It rode over my grocery basket. It stayed at the foot of my bed at night. I had an awareness that when it broke, my future would be revealed.

I didn't know any Pentecostal people in the city where I was living. I didn't have a Pentecostal friend or minister to talk to. I was alone in my new walk with God and didn't know what had happened to me. God, in His sovereign mercy, dropped a cloud over me, and it stayed there for weeks.

The night it broke, I was ministering in Atlanta, Georgia. As I left the service and returned to my room the cloud hovered over me. I laid down on my bed and started praising the Lord. As I lay under the cloud it began to burst. Immediately, I began to laugh and continued laughing for some time. I could not stop laughing. I was a guest in a home and didn't want to disturb my hosts, so I stuck a pillow in my mouth. I didn't know there was such a thing as laughter in the Spirit. I didn't know there could be such joy in the Lord.

I was grieving from the recent loss of almost all my family, through the same genetic bone disease I had just been healed of. I had lived for some time at the point of death from that disease. Until Jesus healed me and baptized me with His Spirit, I didn't know you could have joy.

The presence of that cloud permeated the house and woke up my hostess. Sensing the presence of God, she went all over the house trying to "find" it. Finally, she knocked on my door, and said, "Is it in here?"

Laughing and crying at the same time, I answered, "Come on in." I laughed and cried for the rest of the night and all the next day.

The next evening at about six o'clock, my hostess said, "I need to help you get dressed. You are supposed to preach in about an hour." I was still laughing. This Methodist professor had flipped.

As I entered the church, the pastor whispered to his son-in-law, "I knew I was supposed to bring her down here to minister. I knew God was going to do something for her. She is going to be all right now." Then he added, "Revelation will be hers — God has gotten hold of her."

When it was time for me to preach, I started to read the Scriptures. I could not read — all I could do was laugh and cry. But the people rushed to the altar until it was full. I didn't have to preach a sermon; the presence of the Lord as He filled me drew the people to Him.

Power of Joy

I am told that laughter was a large part of the revival of 1948. It is a part of the move of God today. I know that some people may try to counterfeit this experience. But that doesn't mean that joy and laughter are not real experiences in God.

I preached recently on the joy of the Lord. I had no idea what the response would be. When I finished preaching, we sang a chorus about the joy of the Lord. The glory of God began to breathe through the church. I saw men bending over in laughter. Children were giggling and teenagers were cackling. I elbowed my husband and said, "It is happening." No one had suggested anything or forced that manifestation of joy happen. The presence of the Lord was simply filling the people and allowing them to experience His joy without inhibition.

We have lived a sour Christianity long enough. When God brings revival this time, we are going to be so happy that we will harass people with our happiness. They will be provoked to jealousy over our carefree, joyful countenances, attitudes and actions.

Joy is not found in worldly pursuits. Most people in the world have already discovered that truth. As the world sees our joy in the Holy Spirit, they will be attracted to God. And, as the presence of God reveals the compassionate heart of Jesus, we will be moved with love toward the unsaved.

Thirteen

COMPASSION

The Heart of Jesus

But when he [Jesus] saw the multitudes, he was moved with compassion on them, because they fainted, and were scattered abroad, as sheep having no shepherd (Matt. 9:36).

One Sunday morning while we were worshipping in the church I pastored in Dallas, Texas, the Holy Spirit told me we should sing "Where the Healing Waters Flow." At the time we were in the midst of high praise music, and I knew suggesting this song would bring a drastic change to the mood of the service. However, the impression was so strong I went to my worship leader and whispered, "Lead the people in 'Where the Healing Waters Flow.'" Quickly, he brought the chorus we were singing to an end and directed the orchestra to begin the song I had suggested.

As soon as we started to sing, a young mother ran out the back door of the sanctuary like an arrow shot out of a bow.

Soon she was back, holding her three-year-old son in her arms.

Her story was a sad one. She had married a brilliant young lawyer, and they had two children. He was adamant against the ways of God. In his intelligence, he felt that religion was beneath him. As his wife turned to God completely, trying to serve Him faithfully, she suffered the disintegration of her marriage through divorce. Her husband left her, taking most of their financial assets with him. She had little income and was struggling financially but remained faithful to the Lord.

I did not know that earlier in the week she had taken her son to the doctor for tests. He had been diagnosed with a form of muscular dystrophy which progressed rapidly. The doctor had predicted it would cripple him totally within a few weeks. It would take his life ultimately.

After receiving the doctor's report she went home and fell on her knees, crying out to God. She said, "Lord, you promised to be my husband. I have no one else to take care of me. Please tell me what to do for my son."

The Lord spoke to her in that moment: "Doris, on Sunday morning when the church sings, 'Where the Healing Waters Flow,' I will heal your son."

I knew none of this when the Holy Spirit spoke to me to sing that song. But this mother came running up to the platform with her boy and thrust him into my arms. As she did, my heart melted within me, and something like liquid fire ran out of my being, through my arms into that little boy. I felt as if my life had poured into him in that instant. I didn't know what the Lord was doing, but I felt His power flowing from me into that body. I put the boy down and said to him, "Come, Chris, run with Pastor."

Many in the congregation who were aware of his situation began shouting. We ran across the platform and back. As we returned to his mother, she volunteered her story. She told me that a few days ago he could not run like that, and then informed me of the doctor's diagnosis and the impending prognosis. The compassion of God that we experienced that morning brought healing to that little boy.

Recently I received a letter from this family, with a picture of Chris. He is now a pro-football player. He is a living testimony to the compassion of God that he received that Sunday morning as a little boy.

I have not felt that strong compassion many times in my life, but when I have, it has always had life-changing effects.

Compassion Defined

There is no other subject more difficult for me to articulate than that of compassion. It is so difficult to find expression in human words for this divine emotion. The Scriptures describe Jesus' response to the needs of people by repeatedly using the phrase "moved with compassion."

The Greek word for compassion is *eleeo*. It means "to show kindness or assistance."[1] Far greater than simply feeling a depth of pity or sympathy, it is a divine force expressed in a deep yearning over the suffering of another. In that divine force there is not only desire to help, but the ability to help as well. We could call it "projected love," which is the real meaning of *agape* — God's divine love. It is love that is focused on a specific area of need for a person or group of people.

Godly compassion springs from the deepest part of our

beings. The Scriptures refer to "bowels of compassion" (1 John 3:17), speaking of our spirits, or our "inner man." When Paul expressed his love for the Philippians he declared: "For God is my record, how greatly I long after you all in the bowels of Jesus Christ" (Phil. 1:8). Such compassion, flowing out of the deepest recesses of our being, will affect and motivate our lives. The psalmist David referred to his spirit as the "reins" of his life (Ps. 26:2). As the reins on a horse guide his direction and actions, so God's compassion will guide the direction and actions of our lives.

All these pictures place the source of compassion on a deeper plane than a fleeting, momentary feeling of pity or sympathy for another. They refer to the spirit of the believer from which the compassion of the Holy Spirit flows freely.

Compassion is the loving outreach of God to the person who needs His touch. When His agape love touches a person, it sets that person free. Bitterness, past hurts, offenses, emotional scars, physical problems, mental bondages and relational difficulties are healed when the divine force of His compassion touches a life.

Counterfeit Compassion

Satan tries to counterfeit everything that God's love does. Many people project a loving attitude toward others with the ulterior motive of gaining their favor. The New Age movement projects a loving face, tolerating everyone's beliefs and opinions, but it refuses to accept God's absolute standards. It is a soulish counterfeit for the love of God.

The counterfeit of compassion originates in the mind and is exercised as mind control. In reality it is witchcraft.

Unfortunately, it is found not only in the secular world but is practiced by some Christians in ministry to gain advantage over people.

True compassion is birthed in our spirits by the Holy Spirit. It causes us to reach out to the needy who cannot give anything in return. Struggling in their pain, these hurting people need a touch of God that will bring wholeness to their bodies, souls and spirits. There is transforming power in the compassion that comes from God, working through a believer.

Compassion and the Anointing

Compassion is not the force that completes the healing but that which energizes the miraculous power of God to begin His work. The supernatural power that performs the miracle is the anointing. Jesus declared this fact when He stood in the synagogue to read the Scriptures: "The Spirit of the Lord is upon me, because he hath anointed me to preach the gospel to the poor; he hath sent me to heal the broken-hearted, to preach deliverance to the captives, and recovering of sight to the blind, to set at liberty them that are bruised" (Luke 4:18). The anointing of the Holy Spirit empowered Jesus to perform miracles for men and women as He was moved in compassion for them.

The anointing may be defined simply as the supernatural power of God that is resident in a believer's spirit by the Holy Spirit. It is the source of the actual power to accomplish God's miraculous work. Jesus promised to give the disciples the *dunamis* power of the Holy Spirit after His ascension: "But ye shall receive power, after that the Holy Ghost is come upon you" (Acts 1:8). *Dunamis* means "force, a miraculous power."[2] That is the inherent, divine ability of the Holy Spirit working through us as He fills us with His anointing.

The anointing operates in its fullness when motivated by God's love, though it can flow through us in a measure despite our lack of love. The apostle Paul taught that the energizing force behind faith is love (Gal. 5:6b). The catalyst for the *dunamis* power which releases faith is that yearning and caring compassion of God. It releases the power of the grace gifts needed to produce the miracle. Projected love or compassion is the motivation for the tangible, supernatural power — or anointing — which effects the miracle.

Love Motivation

After Paul gives detailed instructions concerning the value and use of spiritual gifts, he declares: "And yet shew I unto you a more excellent way" (1 Cor. 12:31). His famous "love chapter" follows — the New Testament portrait of a Christian. He concludes his description of divine love by repeating that we should desire spiritual gifts, but we are to pursue love above all.

Love purifies our desire for the power of God. There is an inherent desire in human nature to rule, though not for godly reasons. Some Christians have even tapped into the power of God without pure motives, using it to satisfy their personal desires for aggrandizement or control.

So few miracles are being worked through Spirit-filled believers, because the energizing force of compassion is not the motivation for attempting many miracles. One of the primary functions of the Holy Spirit is to shed the love of God abroad in our hearts (Rom. 5:5). If He is working in our hearts, the result will be a divine compassion for others.

Cold Love

An overwhelming love for God and one another accompanies our initial baptism in the Holy Spirit. That love motivates our words, attitudes and actions in positive ways. However, if we face the trials of life without allowing the Holy Spirit to continue to fill us with Himself, love often grows cold. Cold love is powerless to energize faith. Therefore, we cannot release the anointing that is within.

Jesus warned that cold love would be a sign of the end times: "And because iniquity shall abound, the love of many shall wax cold" (Matt. 24:12). Cold love makes ministers and believers ineffective. We cannot manufacture divine love — it is not a product of soul power. God sheds it abroad in our hearts by the Holy Ghost. As we seek Him in obedience, He will be faithful to fill us with His divine love.

Compassion and Character

An overwhelming compassion, a baptism of love poured out from Christ Himself to His people, will accompany the last great move of God upon the earth. It shall come in ever-increasing waves — Christ's deep, fulfilling love flowing in us and through us in compassion to others.

How can we show that Jesus lives and walks through us if we don't walk in love? Unfortunately, many charismatic Christians have forsaken the pursuit of character in their pursuit of charisma, anointing, power and the gifts of the Spirit.

They do not walk in love. The love of God is the channel through which the Holy Spirit works. He doesn't work through our giftings alone — He works through love.

Compassion Through Relationship

When was the last time you heard your heavenly Father say, "My child, I love you"?

How long has it been since you crawled onto His lap, looked into His eyes and called him "daddy"? When was your worship so powerful that you knew you were exchanging intimacies of love with the living God? Have you felt His love in such a way that spoke to Him in the love language of the Shulamite girl in the Song of Solomon? A relationship like that will open our hearts to receive the depths of God's compassion.

Have you ever put your arms around someone to pray for them and felt the love of God well up inside you for them? Have you ever felt the divine force that is an impartation of God into another person? When that happens, the Christ-life within you has reached out, pouring Himself into another and lifting them with His divine presence. That impartation of God's compassion is greater than spiritual gifts. It is the love of God Himself, moving from you to that person.

The alcoholic, the adulterer and the blasphemer has had enough church rules and restrictions. Nothing will change a person as quickly as pouring the divine compassion of Christ into them through a loving word or a loving touch in spite of their appearance. In that way, the living Word becomes a Person — reaching out to those who can see Him in no other way.

The miracle of salvation won't happen by memorizing verses of Scripture or presenting four spiritual laws. Church programs won't produce change — but projected love will.

As the holiness of God changes our character, we will touch others with the true compassion of God and see lives changed. Everyone that Jesus touched was changed. The Church is going to take Jesus to the world and hear people exclaim, "Someone touched me — I'm not the same anymore." The ministry of impartation belongs to the body of Christ.

This next move of God won't bring sinners to us — we will go to them as Jesus taught in His parable of the great supper. When the guests who were first invited to the master's great feast made excuses, the master of the house became angry and told his servant, "Go out quickly into the streets and lanes of the city, and bring in hither the poor, and the maimed, and the halt, and the blind" (Luke 14:21b).

The servant obeyed, and still there was room at the table. So the master commanded the servant to "go out into the highways and hedges, and compel them to come in, that my house may be filled" (Luke 14:23). This is a picture of the Father's heart. He has prepared a wonderful banquet and longs for His house to be full.

Do we share His heart? When was the last time we wept over the plight of a homosexual or a drug addict? Are we moved with compassion to help a homeless child or a young girl who is having an abortion? Do we see the child abuser, rapist or murderer through the compassionate, loving eyes of God? Do we believe God can change completely the lives of people involved in willful, malicious sin?

It is only as God imparts His divine life to us, Spirit to

spirit, and impregnates us with His divine life and compassion that we can. When that happens, we will not be content to stay within our church walls. We will be compelled to go to the streets to find those who are hurting and wounded and take the love of God to them. Out of us will flow the divine love of God — the true "agape" force that brought Jesus to the earth to save mankind.

I don't know how long I will live, but above all else I want to leave a legacy of love with the Church — a hunger for relationship with Jesus that cannot be satisfied by anyone but Him. When you come to Jesus in prayer, do you always ask for something? Do you ask for your needs to be met? Do you want to display a gift or exercise power? Just come to worship Him. Let Him pour His compassion into your life.

As His compassion fills us we will see the prayer of Jesus fulfilled: "That they may be one, even as we are one" (John 17:22b).

Fourteen

UNITY

Jesus' Prayer Answered

> That they all may be one; as thou, Father, art in
> me, and I in thee, that they also may be one in
> us: that the world may believe that thou hast sent
> me (John 17:21).

Unity is the greatest challenge facing the Church today
as we seek to advance God's kingdom in the earth.
Yet unity in the Church is essential to satisfy the
heart of God and to fulfill His purposes in the earth. Jesus
prayed that all who would believe on Him would become one.
He knew that unity was the priority of the Father's heart.

Unity Defined

Unity is the state of being made one. It means to have "a
oneness of mind, or feeling, as when people live in concord,
harmony, or agreement."[1] Unity does not preclude diversity,

as the Scriptures are careful to explain. Metaphors and allegories in the Bible that describe the redeemed people of God depict a community characterized by unity with diversity and diversity in unity. For example, the Bible describes diversities of manifestations and gifts, but one Spirit (1 Cor. 12:4). Unity is not uniformity, nor is diversity division.

The apostle Paul illustrates the divine purpose for the unity and diversity of Christ's body by referring to the human body. As we mentioned earlier, he explains that the human body has many members with different functions, all necessary to the health of the body. He then exhorts, however, that while the gifts and ministries in the Church vary, they must not be allowed to cause division by drawing attention to the gifted person or creating "cliques" within the Church.

Paul insists that the redeemed community is one organic whole consisting of diverse members. That diversity is intended to bring a divine variety of ministry to the whole body of Christ for the common good of all. A beautiful picture emerges when we envision a body of people, all variously gifted by the Holy Spirit, ministering in love to one another. As the Church leaves the immaturity of competition, and manifests maturity of unity in Christian compassion, she will become a witness to the whole world.

The body of Christ cannot endure competition between its members. We need each other if we are going to fulfill God's divine purpose in this earth. When we fail to flow with every other member of the body, we are rebelling against God's purpose for His corporate body and are defeating our own personal destiny. We are injuring other members in the body and withholding the beautiful, corporate Christ that God desires to manifest to the world.

Here is the supreme glory of the Christian man: He is part of the body of Christ on earth. I believe with all my heart that this next move of God is going to bring the Church into a greater unity than we have ever known before. The Holy Spirit is going to reveal Jesus Christ to the world through the Church: "To Him be glory in the Church" (Eph. 3:21a).

Dashed Hopes of Unity

Unfortunately, unity is more easily defined than attained, as the history of mankind and the Church reveals. During the charismatic renewal, many thought unity had come to the Church because of the thousands of people from all denominations who were receiving the baptism of the Holy Spirit. Even secular newspapers wrote favorable articles about the "glossolalia movement" bringing together Christians of all denominations.[2]

While I was traveling in Jerusalem during the time of that renewal, I met David du Plessis, who was instrumental in bringing many denominational leaders together, including Catholics. When he found out I was a Methodist minister and professor, he invited me to consider ministering with him. He talked about the formation of an ecumenical movement and felt we would be able to witness to our denominational friends concerning the baptism of the Holy Spirit. Though I was unable to accept his invitation, I shared his enthusiasm for bringing the Church together. We both had high hopes for unity in the body of Christ at that time.

But before long we realized that the Church had begun not only to split, but to splinter as well, even during the charismatic renewal. Some groups followed ministries that had the manifestation of being "slain in the Spirit," while others preferred to follow ministers who "lengthened legs." Though these manifestations were not inherently wrong, they became a means of dividing the Church into different camps. Rather than seeing the unity we had hoped for, we saw the Church divided over these and other issues.

Shortly after the emphasis on these issues had subsided, the Holy Spirit began to renew praise and worship in the Church. He gave many beautiful and anointed songs, and there was a new wave of praise and worship in the Church that extended to many nations. International worship symposiums were established to help share the wonderful truths of praise and worship and to train musicians to flow in this fresh anointing.

I was one of the professors invited to teach praise and worship to thousands of believers who attended these symposiums. As I saw people from every denomination, without name tags, worshipping together, I declared joyfully, "This is it! Surely we must be experiencing the unity in the body of Christ that we have all been waiting for. No one is interested in declaring their affiliation; they are all worshipping Jesus together!"

Sadly, however, it was not long before the Church was splitting again over new issues — whether or not to carry banners, whether dancing was a true form of worship, whether dancing should be choreographed or spontaneous. Songwriters became "stars" to thousands of enthusiastic followers. Some groups followed one personality while other groups supported another. The unity we had hoped to see come to the Church through this wave of praise and worship seemed thwarted once more.

Focus on Jesus

When Jesus stood in the synagogue to read the Scriptures, He declared:

> The Spirit of the Lord is upon me, because he hath anointed me to preach the gospel to the poor; he hath sent me to heal the broken-hearted, to preach deliverance to the captives, and recovering of sight to the blind, to set at liberty them that are bruised, To preach the acceptable year of the Lord (Luke 4:18,19).

After Jesus finished reading, the Scriptures say:

> And the eyes of all them that were in the synagogue were fastened on him, and they wondered at the gracious words which proceeded out of his mouth (Luke 4:20, 22).

Verse 22 reads as follows in the Amplified Bible: "and marveled at the words of grace that came forth from His mouth." The world has not yet heard that message of grace. They didn't hear it in the charismatic renewal because we were expounding "our" spiritual gifts and ministries.

In immaturity, some sought to make a name for themselves through spiritual gifts or doctrinal emphasis. Others looked for renown through Church government or a program of evangelism. Unity will not come to the Church through church programs or forms of government. It will not be a product of human methods or personalities. Unity will come to the body of Christ in this next move of God for one reason — everyone's focus will be on Jesus.

Jesus is going to stand in His Church again and declare: "I have come to heal the brokenhearted, to deliver captives, cause the blind to see, and set at liberty them that are bruised." As the Church begins to walk in unity, healings and miracles will be an everyday occurrence. But they will seem unremarkable in the revelation of Jesus. We won't worry about "our" ministry any longer. His ministry — healing broken lives and setting captives free — will be all that matters. When that happens, the world will look at the Church and exclaim: "Amazing grace!"

The Power of Unity

Unity can be dangerous. When the Golden Gate Bridge in California was restored a few years ago, the media published a warning to the one million people who planned to walk across it the first night it was open. They warned them that if they walked together in rank — in a unified pattern — the bridge would fall from the impact. Marching bands often break cadence when they cross a bridge. That is a natural example of the power that spiritual unity can bring when the Church walks together as one man.

Unity will make the Church a powerful force in the earth. Jesus declared that the world would know the Father had sent Him as believers became one in Them (John 17:21). Perhaps He gave us the greatest key to true evangelism in that statement. There is a power in unity that will draw the world to Jesus.

Unity in Type

The Scriptures are filled with admonitions for believers to live in unity, both in the Old and New Testaments.[3] The psalmist, David, extolled the virtues and blessings of a unified people when he wrote:

> Behold how good and how pleasant it is for brethren to dwell together in unity! It is like the precious ointment upon the head, that ran down upon the beard, even Aaron's beard: that went down to the skirts of his garments; As the dew of Hermon, and as the dew that descended upon the mountains of Zion: for there the Lord commanded the blessing, even life for evermore (Ps. 133:1-3).

David's analogy of unity here was one the Old Testament saints understood very well. They were familiar with the anointing oil that Moses poured upon Aaron to set him apart for service in the tabernacle. They knew a priest had the responsibility of living in unity with God and man in order to understand and administer holy things.

The holy anointing oil was composed of four major spices: myrrh, cinnamon, cassia and sweet calamus, all mixed together in a large quantity of olive oil (Ex. 30:22-25). It typifies the Holy Spirit, while each ingredient speaks to us of the bitter and the sweet.[4] Even as we cultivate our relationship with God, we find that life is full of bitter as well as sweet experiences. Jesus, our High Priest, the Head of the Church, certainly experienced both bitter and sweet in His life. Yet, even in His deepest suffering, He maintained communion with God and companionship with His brothers.[5]

Anointing the Head

The application of the anointing oil is a biblical type of unity. Following that type, we can understand that unity begins at the head, for the anointing oil was poured upon the head of Aaron. Jesus is the Head of the Church, and believers are to form the body of Christ. As the Church experiences this anointing, it will walk in a spirit of unity that crosses denominational lines, cultural barriers, prejudice, customs and any other issue that presently causes divisions.

God calls His leaders to unity first. The anointing for unity will begin at the head. As undershepherds of the flock of God, pastors will follow Jesus' example of oneness with the Father and learn to walk in unity with each other before they lead their people to do the same. The spirit of competition must be replaced with a divine spirit of cooperation in order for Jesus' prayer to be answered and for the world to recognize the Church as different from them. I thank God for those who are working to bring reconciliation in the Church, beginning with the leadership.

Anointing the Beard

Continuing with this biblical type, we see that the next area the anointing oil touched was Aaron's beard. In the Jewish culture, the growing of a beard represents manhood and maturity. When the apostle Paul exhorted the Ephesian church to unity in spirit and in faith, he admonished them:

"that we henceforth be no more children, tossed to and fro...but speaking the truth in love, may grow up into him in all things, which is the head, even Christ" (Eph. 4:14-15).

As we mature in Christ we will become seekers of unity, rather than seekers of our own gain. The time is past for believers to seek their own ministries and build their own reputations at the expense of others.

Anointing the Garments

The anointing oil fell from Aaron's beard to the borders of his garments. Bells and pomegranates were sewn onto the borders of the priest's garments, side by side and alternating, so that they touched each other (Ex. 39:25). They represent the gifts and fruit of the Holy Spirit as they should be manifested in the Church. When the priest entered the inner sanctuary he was hidden from the view of the Israelites gathered in the outer court area. As he walked within the inner court, from the table of shewbread to the golden candlestick and back again, the bells would ring (Ex. 29). That sound gave evidence that the priest had not died in the presence of God because of his sin, and that his ministry unto God was acceptable.[6] Each of us needs that anointing to make us acceptable in the presence of God.

The apostle Paul teaches that two things keep us from unity: our carnal natures and the improper use of the gifts of the Holy Spirit. He told the Corinthians: "The testimony of Christ was confirmed in you: so that ye come behind in no gift; waiting for the coming of our Lord Jesus Christ" (1 Cor. 1:6-7). Yet there were attitudes of competition among them that caused them to be divided (1 Cor. 1:10). He said they were carnal and immature, calling them babes (1 Cor. 3:1).

Even today the gifts of the Spirit, given to the Church to edify and build us together, too often can become a cause of disunity when we use them to build our own "kingdoms." Like the Corinthians, the very gifts the Spirit gives us to bring us into maturity and unity can be used to separate us as we struggle to become mature. Out of immaturity, we operate in the gifts of the Holy Spirit as if they originated with us, forgetting that all that we have comes from Him and is for Him.

The diversities of gifts and callings given to believers are for the purpose of exalting Christ and building His Church. We need the anointing of God to flow to our garments, touch our gifts, and bring death to our carnal nature, that we might bear the fruit of the Spirit.

Place of Refreshing

The psalmist continues to describe unity as a place of pleasantness and refreshing. He said it was like the dew on Mount Hermon (Ps. 133:3). Dew is that refreshing moisture so welcome after the heat of the sun has subsided. The dew falls at night when all creation is resting and natural elements are at peace. Dew represents restfulness in the kingdom of God that the Holy Spirit came to give.[7]

I wonder if we realize the time and energy consumed by churches as they work to put out "brush fires" caused by carnal competitions. The effort could be put to better use by igniting the flames of the Holy Spirit that would enlighten this darkened world. The enemy energizes our petty differences. He knows the power of unity in the Church and fears it exceedingly.

David refers specifically to the dew of Mount Hermon,

one of the highest peaks in the mountainous region east of the Jordan River.[8] Is not the Church destined to be the highest, most influential place in our society? It is to represent to the world a place of restfulness from competition and division, a place filled with love and cooperation. Only the spirit of unity will exalt the Church to its rightful place and cause the world to look to it for refuge.

Unity in Crisis

The attacks of the enemy that we have discussed have all hindered the unity of the Church in specific ways. Unresolved offense, for example, makes us vulnerable to the Absalom spirit, opening us to the spirit of betrayal against God's anointed leadership. However, God is cleansing the Church of these hindrances to unity and preparing her to reign in the power of that unity that only Christ can bring. Besides these attacks, there is another internal cause for disunity that must be understood so that that we can be cleansed from its consequences.

Racism is one of the greatest crises facing the world and affecting the unity of the Church today. Racism is not a demon or even a principality — it is a world ruler. This powerful ruling spirit sets itself up in the natural mind of man as an authority on what is right and wrong. It employs even the spirit of death and murder in its verdicts.

The Basis of Racism

There are two fundamental aspects to racism: pride and fear. Judging that those who are different from us are inferior is the ultimate form of pride. The Scriptures declare that God is opposed to the proud but gives grace to the humble (James 4:6). Fear, the second aspect of racism, is a result of mankind's insecurity because of the fall of man that resulted in his separation from God. The insecure are afraid of those who are different from them; those whom they cannot control. These powerful and deeply interwoven attitudes of pride and fear that permeate all of society makes it vulnerable to racism.

The world is about to lose control of its racial problems. In reality, racism is a spiritual problem that no legislation or human authority can control or resolve. If the Church does not face the problem of racism and overcome it within herself, the world will soon fall into an abyss of chaos, destruction and suffering of unprecedented proportions.

God's Remedy for Racism

The apostle Paul declared in his day that the greatest racial barrier — the division between Jews and Gentiles — was overcome in Christ. He wrote: "There is neither Jew nor Greek, there is neither bond nor free, there is neither male nor female: for ye are all one in Christ Jesus" (Gal. 3:28). The love of Christ eradicates racial barriers that produce hatred and prejudice, establishing a new standard for right and wrong.

The death of Jesus on the cross broke down the walls between Jews and Gentiles, abolishing enmity and reconciling both groups of people unto God (see Eph. 2:11-17). Only as we accept the sacrifice of the blood of Jesus will we know deliverance from that same kind of enmity between races. The power of the cross deals fundamentally with both the pride of man and his fear.

It is the work of the Holy Spirit to convict the world of sin. Though this convicting work brings a painful revelation of our sins, it causes us to run willingly to the cross to find grace and forgiveness. There our pride is destroyed as we recognize our dependency on the cross. With our intimacy with God restored, we are cleansed from fear, for "perfect love casteth out fear" (1 John 4:18). The deeper the work of the cross in us, the more humble and secure we will be in His love.

When we, who had become so removed from the character of God, are grafted back into Him, receiving His nature, a profound appreciation invades us for those who are different from us. We judge people from a spiritual perspective, not after the flesh or external standards. As Paul stated: "Therefore...we recognize no man according to the flesh" (2 Cor. 5:16a, NAS). The Church, above any other community, should not judge people according to the color of their skin or their cultural background. We must be governed by a biblical perspective, and judge all by the Spirit.

Results of Unity

Unity attracts people. Everyone wants to be on a united team. The world knows that unity is impossible for people who are bent on making a name for themselves. We need only look at the current problems among high-paid, superstar athletes to recognize this fact. The world will recognize the difference unity makes to the chaos of personal ambition and one-upmanship.

Living in unity brings a refreshing, revitalizing force to our lives, in part simply because we have been relieved of the tension created by competing with others. But there is also a refreshing because the Lord has promised to command His blessing in the place of unity. The psalmist ended his description of unity by saying: "For there the Lord commanded the blessing, even life forevermore" (Ps. 133:3b). Unity brings the blessing of the Lord to our lives and that gives us a foretaste of heaven.

Jesus ended His prayer with the cry, "that the love wherewith thou hast loved me may be in them, and I in them" (John 17:26). In this prayer, He expressed His desire that we enjoy relationship with the Father as He knows it, and that we would see His glory. As we learn to walk in unity in the Church, we will come to a new revelation of Jesus, and subsequently, of the Father.

Fifteen

JESUS IN THE CHURCH

A Revelation of the Father

He that loveth me shall be loved of my Father,
and I will love him, and will manifest myself to
him (John 14:21).

We do not have to wait until heaven to see the glory
of God in the Church. The glory of God will be
seen as Jesus reveals Himself in our human temples of clay. In this next move of God, the glory of God is
going to fill the lives of believers, and all the world will see it.

The Scriptures declare that it is the work of the Holy Spirit
to reveal Jesus to us and in us. Jesus told His disciples: "When
he, the Spirit of truth is come, he will guide you into all
truth...He shall glorify me: for he shall receive of mine, and
shall show it unto you" (John 16:13-14). The apostle Paul
taught that we are the temple of God and that the Spirit of God
dwells in us (1 Cor. 3:16). Without the working of the Holy

Spirit in us, we cannot know Jesus, who is Truth. In this next move of God, as the Holy Spirit works to reveal Jesus in us, the Church is going to see Jesus as she has not seen Him before. And the glory of God is going to be revealed in the Church.

Where Is the Glory?

When God made mankind, He made him a tripartite being — one with a spirit, a soul and a body (1 Thess. 5:23; Heb. 4:12). He did not intend for there to be a "veil of flesh" separating man's spirit from his soul. We know that God is a Spirit. Before mankind disobeyed God in the garden, Adam and Eve communed with God, spirit to Spirit. He communicated His words of life through their spirits to their souls. When that communion was broken through deception and disobedience, man's spirit died. This "death" did not destroy the spirit, but it broke man's relationship with God. It was then that man's soul — his mind, emotions and will — began to rule him apart from relationship with God, under the influence of sin.

When we are born again unto salvation, the Spirit of God restores our spirits so that we can be in communion with Him, and we become temples of the Spirit of God. As it says in Ephesians 2:1, we were "dead in trespasses and sins" and He quickens us. Once again, we are made alive to God. However, because our psyches have been so enslaved to the power of sin, there is a veil of flesh between our recreated spirit, where Jesus dwells, and our carnal mind, emotions and will. It is as though the veil of the temple that was torn in two when Jesus died must be torn again inside of us — His temples — in order to allow Christ free access to them.

Only the Word of God can do the supernatural work

required to rend that veil inside of us. The Scriptures declare that the "Word of God is quick, and powerful, and sharper than any two-edged sword, piercing even to the dividing asunder of soul and spirit, and of the joints and marrow, and is a discerner of the thoughts and intents of the heart" (Heb. 4:12). As we choose to obey the Word of God, it acts as a knife to cut away the veil of flesh that hides the life of Christ within our spirits. Yielding to the working of the Holy Spirit in our lives and allowing our self-life to be crucified through the dealings of God will allow Jesus to fill His temple. When this work of the Holy Spirit is complete, we will see the glory of God in the Church, as Paul declared it: "Christ in you, the hope of glory" (Col. 1:27).

Because we have kept the Christ-life in us "locked up" in our spirits, not allowing our self-life to be crucified, we have not known Jesus as we should have known Him. The "cave" dealings of God that bring us to obedience to the Word will cause the life of Christ to develop in us. His glory will fill our temples to the degree that we give up our self-life in exchange for the Christ-life. As that happens, we will become holy and know divine joy and compassion, learning to walk in unity with our fellow believers.

That is not the state of the Church at present. Though the incorruptible seed of eternal life has been planted in her, the Church has not yet matured to the place of revelation that allows her to know Jesus as God has intended. Some may not even understand the continuing work of revelation, believing the written Word provides the total revelation of Christ. There is much more involved in knowing Jesus than mentally grasping facts about His life or even expounding truths that He taught.

What Is Revelation?

A simple definition of revelation is this: disclosing a divine truth that has been hidden. For Christians, it involves the unveiling of the Christ that already lives in our spirits. In my book, *Presenting the Holy Spirit, Who Is He?* (Vol. 1), I state:

> The Spirit of Truth takes us through a divine learning process to make revelation a reality that changes our lives. That process results in the unveiling of the Christ who is in us…The Word reveals the veil of flesh in our lives that keeps Christ so hidden that we do not know Him as we should. 'Line upon line' the Spirit of Truth works to remove that veil of flesh to reveal Christ in us until His glory, His divine Presence, fills us.
>
> Paul declared that we are the temple of the Holy Spirit (1 Cor. 3:16). As the Holy Spirit fills our temple, the mind of Christ becomes our mind, His emotions become our emotions, and His will becomes our will. Our will becomes His will, and we become the will of God. It is God's desire for His manifest presence to completely fill His temples.
>
> The first step toward revelation in this divine process is to receive *information*. We must first receive a basic truth in our minds in order for the Holy Spirit to bring it to our remembrance.
>
> When that information begins to be a light to our spirits, it becomes *illumination*. We understand, in a way we never understood before, the truth that was once only information to us.

The Holy Spirit (in us) receives the Word with joy and, as we receive it from Him, it becomes *inspiration* to us. New desires to obey the Word fill our hearts.

When that transcribed Word moves from our heads to our hearts, it becomes a living Word to us as *revelation*. Revelation makes the truth become a living Person to us and in us.

After revelation begins to work in our hearts, the next step in this divine process is *realization,* understanding that we are being changed through our obedience to the revelation that has become a part of our life.

A consistent walk in greater depth of revelation then brings a gradual *transformation* to our lives. We are changed from glory to glory into the image of the Son through our obedience to that revelation.

The final step the Spirit of Truth works in us is the *manifestation* of Jesus' character in our lives. Maturity is the beauty of Jesus seen in people who have allowed the Spirit of Truth to touch their lives in every area of their soul and spirit. They, in obedience to God, have continually turned from sin and allowed the nature of Christ to be fully unveiled in them.[1]

Glory Revealed Through Suffering

The life of Christ will be revealed in us as we are victorious in the trials we endure. Paul understood this when he wrote, "For I reckon that the sufferings of this present time are not worthy to be compared with the glory which shall be revealed in us" (Rom 8:18). He explained to the Corinthians that believers are changed from glory to glory by the Spirit of the Lord (2 Cor. 3:18). Then he described many difficult trials he was experiencing, and declared: "For this momentary, light affliction is producing for us an eternal weight of glory far beyond all comparison" (2 Cor. 4:17, NAS).

As Jesus is seen in the Church through mature believers, once again the presence of God will fill the temple as He did in the Old Testament. Only this time, the temple will be God's own creation — mankind — as He originally intended when He created Adam. The Church will march triumphantly as one man in the world, filled with the glory of the Lord.

The prophet Habakkuk saw clearly the day when "the earth shall be filled with the knowledge of the glory of the Lord, as the waters cover the sea" (Hab. 2:14). He was seeing prophetically the "glorious Church, not having spot, or wrinkle, or any such thing; but that it should be holy and without blemish" (Eph. 5:27). And it was Paul who declared that for this reason Christ gave Himself for the Church, "that he might sanctify and cleanse it with the washing of water by the word" (Eph. 5:26). In this next move of God, Jesus will be revealed fully in the Church as individual believers allow Jesus to be revealed in them. Then we shall experience the greatest revelation of all — a revelation of the Father.

A Revelation of the Father

Everything that Jesus did was for the purpose of revealing

the Father to us. Jesus said, "The works which the Father hath given me to finish, the same works that I do, bear witness of me, that the Father hath sent me" (John 5:36). He did nothing of Himself, out of His own will or desire, but only those things He saw the Father doing (John 5:30). Every parable was intended to reveal the love of the Father. Every miracle He performed was to show the Father. When He prayed for Lazarus to be raised from the dead, Jesus said to His Father, "And I knew that thou hearest me always: but because of the people which stand by I said it, that they may believe that thou hast sent me" (John 11:42).

Still, while Jesus was on earth, even His disciples failed to grasp the revelation of the Father. When they asked Jesus to show them the Father, Jesus' asked poignantly: "Have I been so long with you, and yet hast thou not known me, Philip? He that hath seen me hath seen the Father" (John 14:9). Was Jesus a failure? Did He fail to communicate to His own disciples the reason for His coming? No. Jesus' ministry to those disciples did not end with His ascension into heaven. He instructed them to wait for the day of Pentecost.

After they were baptized in the Holy Spirit, the disciples were empowered to become the Church. Though they turned the world upsidedown with the gospel of Christ, they still did not have a clear revelation of the Father. It was Paul the apostle who first declared: "Ye have received the Spirit of adoption, whereby we cry, Abba, Father" (Rom. 8:15). The other apostles' later writings reveal their revelation of the Father. John wrote: "And truly our fellowship is with the Father, and with his Son Jesus Christ" (1 John 1:3).

The Church today needs this same empowering and revelation of the Father. If Jesus were standing before us, would He not ask us the same question: "Have I been so long with you and you have not seen the Father?" How long has He lived in us as born-again believers, without our coming to know Him in revelation and power? We need our eyes opened to the reality of God who dwells in us. We need to experience the fellowship with the Father that the disciples testified about.

That is an awesome prospect to me. When that revelation of the Father comes, we will confess that we have not known God. We say He is our Father, and we know He forgave us. But, in the revelation that is coming, we are going to know the Father's love in its fullness, with all the peace, security, well-being, hope and comfort that He is. As we focus our eyes on Jesus, we will come to know the Father, for the Scriptures declare that Jesus is the "brightness of his glory, and the express image of his person" (Heb. 1:3).

Jesus will not fail His Church; He came to reveal to us the Father. As we begin to receive this revelation, our eyes will no longer be on gifts, ministries or how much faith we have. Our eyes will be fastened on Jesus. His holiness will be our nature, and the Church will be filled with joy that is motivated by compassion. We will march together in unity — in divine fellowship with our Father.

Chapter 16

THE GLORIOUS CHURCH REVEALED
The End of the Next Move of God

This world is going to see the Church come out of hiding, no longer "cave dwellers" in training. The day will soon dawn when the Spirit will say, "Arise, shine; for thy light is come, and the glory of the Lord is risen upon thee" (Is. 60:1). It will not matter that darkness covers the earth, and gross darkness the people, for the glory of the Lord will be seen upon us — His Church in the earth.

The true Church in these days of testing and training is being transformed from pitiful impotence into a powerful influence in the earth as the Holy Spirit reveals

Christ in His glory through the lives of believers. The Church is going to move in power to bring people to Christ, the living Word.

This glorious Church will set the pace, demand respect and again hold a high reputation for godliness and holiness. It will be a remnant, not in the sense of a small number, but in the sense of being distinctive in character, separate from the false Church. Remnant refers to a special people, protected from destruction (Zeph. 2:7,9; Rev. 12:17). As the glory of God shines through Christ's Church, protecting her from destruction, she will be God's instrument to speak to the world before Christ's return.

The Breaking Light of Dawn

I have witnessed in many churches the attack of the enemy in the form of a Jezebel spirit or the betrayal of an Absalom. I have seen the destruction of the pseudo-counseling spirit in some churches and the tyranny of the pharisaical spirit in others. I have wept and prayed with heartbroken pastors and leaders who felt their lives and ministries were destroyed.

In recent months some of these pastors have called to tell me about the mighty visitation of God they are now experiencing in their churches. They are experiencing the power of God in worship and praise, in fresh revelation of the Word, in renewed zeal in their personal lives and in the lives of their churches, as well as in numerical growth. They are seeing the light of God arise upon them as they walk in repentance and forgiveness. They have allowed God to circumcise their hearts so He could bring them into the promised land.

Beginnings of Revival

What joy is filling these ministers and their churches as they open themselves to the fresh visitation of God. Many are experiencing the signs and wonders of laughter and being slain in the Spirit. Believers are giving testimony to emotional and mental healing, restored marriages, a fresh revelation of Jesus and the love of the Father as they lie — sometimes for hours — in the presence of God. Many sense a new compassion for other hurting people.

In my home church in Tennessee, a woman testified that as she lay in the presence of God He showed her that her faith for healing had been shipwrecked. She is a mature intercessor in the church who has offered loyal prayer support for many years. But the enemy had used disappointments to shipwreck her faith in praying for healing for herself and others. She wept as she shared how the Spirit of God had shown her step by step how her faith had been hindered, yet did not leave her with a sense of condemnation. He simply cleansed her and renewed her faith to pray for people's healing. She had never felt the love and compassion of God in such a strong way.

In this same church a middle-aged pharmacist testified that he did not expect ever to have a real relationship with Jesus. He thought he would simply come to church with his family and sit toward the back, hoping to make heaven someday. As he responded to the altar call one Sunday morning, he was standing behind a lady who was slain in the Spirit. He reached out to catch her and found himself falling. For several hours he lay there, unable to get up, as Jesus revealed Himself to him, telling him that He wanted to have a personal relationship with Him. That man has been transformed and today is praying for others to receive this fresh anointing of the Holy Spirit.

Children are experiencing supernatural revelations of Jesus and giving testimony of "visiting heaven" as they lie in God's presence. Some have seen angels and express the happiness of heaven. Others have heard God speak to them about His plan for their lives.[1]

Reports are coming from churches across our nation and from around the world of a new outpouring of the Holy Spirit. Recently my pastor, Sue Curran, ministered in the Christ for the Nations Bible School in Germany and experienced a wave of revival as students were being slain in the Spirit, laughing or weeping, or simply having an encounter with God. In England, denominational churches are seeing this same phenomenon of being slain in the Spirit and filled with joy and laughter.[2] The most important characteristic of this fresh outpouring of the Spirit is the consistent report of radically transformed lives and churches, displaying the love and joy and generosity of God.

Many of these believers have withstood the attacks of

Jezebel and Absalom. They recognized the enemy's counterattack and have ripped off the disguises of the spirits of witchcraft and pharisaism. Their wholeness is the product of revival — not pseudo-counseling techniques. God has chosen to visit His people once again, as He showed me more than thirty years ago that He would do. What we are seeing now is just a beginning of what God is going to do in the months ahead for those who seek His presence.

Removal of Hindrances

God's remnant is not hindered from revival by denominationalism, human tradition, prejudice, culture or customs. The Holy Spirit has breathed truth into their hearts, cleansing them from all that would delay the move of God. Cleansed, confident and prepared, they are actively participating to bring revival to the world.

I was scheduled to speak at the Conference of Third World Revival Churches in Nassau, Bahamas, a few months ago where thousands of leaders and believers were gathered from many nations. As I prepared to go to the platform, I heard the Holy Spirit say to me, "You cannot minister to these people until you repent of the prejudice of your nation against them." I was stunned. How could I address such a sensitive situation? Yet I knew I had heard my Father's voice, and I dared not disobey.

As I was presented to that great congregation, I

opened my mouth and told them what God had just spoken to me. I asked their forgiveness for the prejudice of my own heart and that of my nation. A spirit of reconciliation flowed among all those thousands of people. Men and women from different countries began to repent for their own prejudices, weeping and embracing one another. The love of God filled that large auditorium as the body of Christ experienced a new level of unity.

Redemptive Truths Established

The Church — God's remnant — is established in the realities of the redemptive truths birthed by the charismatic renewal. Out of her life flows spiritual gifts, faith and temporal blessings. Christ Himself has given her His power of attorney, and she carries out His business on earth in that divine authority. That renewal prepared the Church for this next move of God, and we are beginning to see evidences of the glorious Church — a holy Church, cleansed and transformed by the character of God within. Her arms will reach out to all the world with joy, compassion and unity.

Prophetic Admonition

May we as God's people hear the Word of the Lord. This is a special day. This is the appointed time. This is the year for us to break out of our shells. It is the year of realizing the fulfillment of "It shall come to pass in those days." As it was with Elijah on Mount Carmel, so it will be with us. The day that Elijah should build the altar and pray the prayer that would bring fire from heaven had been appointed in advance. It had been foreordained that the prophets of Baal should be destroyed and that once more the glory of the Lord would come upon His people. To a man, they were cut down — those who had lied to and seduced the people of God, lining up in the name of Baal against the ways of the Lord.

We must be careful not to be deceived into following our usual order of worship, saying that we know how to do it or that we have always done it this way. In this next move of God we will not have "church as usual." God's Jehus are ready to receive a fresh anointing to replace the rule of Ahab and Jezebel. They will be filled with zeal to bring down the rulers of darkness. There is a prophetic word on the lips of the Elijahs of today that will feed the flesh of Jezebel to the dogs. They will share the Word of the Lord, and we will hear what the Spirit says to the Church.

These are days when God's Spirit will move upon our altars, causing His fire to fall upon them. We must remember that an altar is what we build, not what God builds. It is our task to place our lives on an altar of consecration; it is God's responsibility to let fire fall upon it. Every person is accountable for building his or her own altar, and everyone shall experience his or her own Mount Carmel.

During David's time of preparation, Saul tried to harm him. Today, as the Sauls of this world are going about doing their mischief, seeking their fame and fortune while asking for prophets to stand with them (as Saul said to Samuel, "Stand with me in this sacrifice"), they are trying to cover their sins rather than repent of them. In contrast to that blatant rebellion, the Davids of today are being prepared to enjoy the character of God as they submit to His circumcision of their hearts from the love of the world and bondage to their self-lives.

Resurrection Power in the Church

Jesus taught the principle of life coming out of death. As we consecrate our lives on the altars we build, God will send the fire and consume us, our bondages and our self-lives. But that is not the end of the matter.

Jesus raised Lazarus from the dead after he was buried for four days. The natural evaluation of his condition was that he "stinketh" (John 11:39). There is much death in the Church today, much burial of that which is stinking. Many times we have yearned in our hearts, as Martha and Mary did, crying, "Had You been here, our brother would not have died" (see John 11:32). We lament, "Lord, if You had brought this next move sooner, our brothers would not have died." We grieve over our family members and church members who have fallen away.

The Lord has promised restoration, raising up a mighty army in the earth. You ask, How can that be possible? How can we expect to see such a resurrection? That question reveals that we have not yet understood

171

the magnitude of the coming revival. The prophet saw this overwhelming flood of revival when he declared, "For the earth will be filled with the knowledge of the glory of the Lord, as the waters cover the sea" (Hab. 2:14, NAS).

The Word of God will come alive to our hearts, and preachers will preach as they have never preached before. They will receive revelation even while they are speaking, declaring that they had not understood these truths before. A great wave of divine revelation knowledge is coming in the next move of God. We will "[taste] the good word of God, and the powers of the world to come" (Heb. 6:5).

In Elijah's day there were seven thousand people hidden in caves who had not "attended church" for a long time. They were kept alive on bread and water as they hid from the wicked Jezebel, who was ruling the land. As this current move of God delivers captives, people will be restored to God and will love the Word again. They will love to praise and worship again.

We may have heard this prophesied years ago, but now it is coming to pass. As members of God's Church in the earth today, we are part of the present fulfillment of His promise to have a glorious church without spot or wrinkle. We declare with the psalmist: "Thou wilt arise and have compassion on Zion; for it is time to be gracious to her, for the appointed time has come" (Ps. 102:13, NAS). Zion in Scripture represents the Church, the people of God, through whom God desires to manifest His presence. It is God's appointed time to favor His people.

National Restoration

When this next move of God begins to bring forth resurrection life, it won't just happen in local churches. It will flow into homes, communities and business places. As it increases, it won't be just droplets of life-giving rain here and there. It will be a flood running to those "in mountains, and in dens and caves of the earth" (Heb. 11:38).

Our government, our church denominations, our social organizations, our school systems, our industries — which have become corrupt, motivated by self-promotion, serving for gold and silver and ruled by covetous practices — will all be changed by the power of God's divine presence. This move of God will be so powerful that throughout our land we will see a return to the great historical foundations of this nation which declare that in God we trust.

Once more people will talk about God as our fathers did. Their conversations will concern the visitation of God rather than the Emmy awards. They will discuss "the riches of the glory of his inheritance in the saints" (Eph. 1:18b) instead of bank accounts, interest rates and retirement programs.

The Church Triumphant

As we believers behold Christ in His glory, we will realize that He has not withheld resurrection life from us. It is sin that has prevented it — unbelief, carnal competition, covetousness and so forth. As we respond to the word of God that is saying, "Build an altar; come in a new surrender of your spirit; come and let Me wash away the cynicism, the criticism, the doubts and unbelief, the fear and weariness of soul," we will hear that sweet sound of heaven as the gates are being raised and the flood begins to pour forth.

I think today I can hear God say, "My people, heaven's windows are opened. The blessings are being poured forth now. They will continue throughout this year, throughout this decade and into the next century. My glory is going to come forth in a continually greater measure." We won't have to say God is moving in Canada, or Florida or California; in England, Germany or Argentina. We will be able to say it is happening right where we are.

God is visiting His people again. The floodgates are about to open, bringing a heaven-sent, gully-washing, sin-killing revival. The Word of the Lord will be fulfilled to us:

> For you will go out with joy, and be led forth with peace; the mountains and the hills will break forth into shouts of joy before you, and all the trees of the field will clap their hands (Is. 55:12, NAS).

The trees of the field are clapping their hands, and the little hills are skipping about. Salvation is come and deliverance is at hand as the prophecies of God's Word are being fulfilled. There will be such a shout of victory that it will be heard to Saul's kingdom, who will fall on his own sword. We won't have to fight the ungodly leaders of the world. God Himself will take care of them. There will be a great toppling. As the walls of Jericho came down with the sound of the trumpet and a shout (Josh. 6:20), so the walls of wickedness in our country are coming down.

There will be a clamping down on violence and wickedness in the media and an end to the destruction wrought by those who stood against marriage and for abortion. The army of God — His Church — is going to march through this nation and bind the powers of darkness, praising the name of our Lord as He releases the spirit of liberty upon our nation.

At present there are little signs of victory here and there as people experience the visitation of God that has caused us to hope again. I believe our hope will increase by leaps and bounds in the days ahead. We will be as the man at the gate Beautiful who came walking and leaping and praising God into the temple (Acts 3:8). We will come in rejoicing in our hearts. As this great move of God breaks forth and the waters I saw in the vision of the hydroelectric plant are released, I believe the Church will become a mighty river that floods the earth until the knowledge of the glory of the Lord covers it.

My admonition to the Church is that no one decide to stay on the bank and observe the debris that a flood inevitably brings. Those who do will declare that this move is not of God because of some who are not walking in it perfectly. We decide whether we will stay with the debris or lift our eyes above it and plunge into the current of God that is going to run fuller, deeper and broader until it covers the earth as the waters cover the sea. It is time to behold Jesus and not be distracted by a few people who do not function properly in the new anointing.

As the Holy Spirit works to revive and restore believers, we are going to see the Church triumphant rise and face her enemies victoriously. This is the revealed destiny of God's people.

Jesus, the Head of the Church, declares: "I will build my church; and the gates of hell shall not prevail against it" (Matt. 16:18). Let us end here by shouting together a more literal translation of that cry: "Move back, gates of hell! Here comes the Church!"

Chapter 1

1. Dr. Fuchsia Pickett, *God's Dream* (Shippensburg, Pa: Destiny Image, 1991), pp. 44-49.
2. W. E. Vine, Merrill F. Unger, William White, Jr., eds., *Vine's Expository Dictionary of Biblical Words* (Nashville, Tenn.: Thomas Nelson Publishers, 1984), s.v. "power."
3. Ibid., s.v. "river."

Chapter 3

1. Francis Frangipane, *The Three Battlegrounds* (Marion, Iowa, 1989), p. 98.
2. Ibid., p. 98.
3. Dick Bernal, *When Lucifer and Jezebel Join Your Church* (Sunnyvale, Calif.: Patson's Press), p. 18.
4. Francis Frangipane, *The Three Battlegrounds* (Marion, Iowa, 1989), p. 98.
5. W. E. Vine, Merrill F. Unger, William White, Jr., eds., *Vine's Expository Dictionary of Biblical Words* (Nashville, Tenn.: Thomas Nelson Publishers, 1984), s.v. "prophecy."

Chapter 5

1. James Strong, "Greek Dictionary of the New Testament," *The New Strong's Exhaustive Concordance of the Bible* (Nashville, Tenn.: Thomas Nelson Publishers, 1984), s.v. "skandalon."
2. Most of my remarks in the section on offense were drawn from: John Bevere, *The Bait of Satan* (Lake Mary, Fla.: Creation House, 1994), pp. 8-14.

Chapter 8

1. "Tradition," *Merriam–Webster's Collegiate Dictionary, 10th Edition* (Springfield, Mass.: Merriam-Webster, Inc., 1993).
2. Christological epistles emphasize Christ, His life and work in us. They include the books of Ephesians, Philipieans, Galatians and Colossians.
3. "Custom," *Merriam–Webster's Collegiate Dictionary, 10th Edition.*

Chapter 9

1. Sue Curran is pastor of Shekinah Ministries, Blountville, Tenn. She is a conference speaker and teacher, and is the author of *Kingdom Principles, The Praying Church, The Forgiving Church* and *The Joshua Generation.*

Chapter 11

1. *Vine's Expository Dictionary of Biblical Words* (Thomas Nelson Publishers, 1984), s.v. "confess, confession."

Chapter 12

1. James Strong, *Strong's Exhaustive Concordance of the Bible* (Nashville, Tenn.: Thomas Nelson Publishers, 1984), s.v. "joy."
2. *Vine's Expository Dictionary of Biblical Words* (Thomas Nelson Publishers, 1984), s.v. "joy."
3. Ibid.

Chapter 13

1. *Vine's Expository Dictionary of Biblical Words* (Nashville, Tenn.: Thomas Nelson Publishers, 1985), s.v. "eleeo."
2. W. E. Vine, Merrill F. Unger, William White, Jr., eds. (Nashville, Tenn.: Thomas Nelson Publishers, 1984), s.v. "power."

Chapter 14

1. *Merriam–Webster's Collegiate Dictionary, Tenth Edition*, s.v. "unity."
2. Since the word "tongue(s)" in the Greek is *glossa,* the charismatic renewal was often labeled the glossolalia movement because so many people spoke in tongues as a result of being baptized by the Spirit. The Greek term *glossai* refers to the gift of speaking in tongues among Spirit-filled believers. (For additional information, see *Nelson's Illustrated Bible Dictionary* (Nashville, Tenn.: Thomas Nelson, 1986), s.v. "tongues" and *The Complete Word Study Dictionary New Testament* by Spiros Zodhiates (Chattanooga, Tenn.: AMG Publishers, 1992), pp. 375-377.)

3. Scriptures referring to unity include: Zech. 2:11; Judg. 20:11; Rom. 6:5; Phil. 2:2; John 17:23; Eph. 4:3,13,16; 1 Cor. 1:10.

4. Dr. Fuchsia Pickett, *Holy Anointing Oil,* Outline Study Series available by writing to: Dr. Fuchsia Pickett, 394 Glory Rd., Blountville, TN 37617.

5. Allen Cook, pastor of Grace Tabernacle, Brentwood, N.H., was a contributor to this study of Aaron's anointing.

6. For more information on the office of the priesthood and the special significance of the priestly garments, see *Vine's Expository Dictionary of Biblical Words* or *Nelson's Bible Dictionary.*

7. Dr. Fuchsia Pickett, *Presenting the Holy Spirit, Who Is He?,* vol. 1 (Shippensburg, Pa.: Destiny Image, 1993), pp. 50-51.

8. *Nelson's Illustrated Bible Dictionary* (Nashville, Tenn.: Thomas Nelson Publishers, 1986), s.v. "mount, mountain."

Chapter 15

1. Dr. Fuchsia Pickett, *Presenting the Holy Spirit, Who Is He?,* vol. 1 (Shippensburg, Pa.: Destiny Image, 1993), pp. 86-89.

2. *Merriam–Webster's Collegiate Dictionary, Tenth Edition,* s.v. "remnant."

Chapter 16

1. Pastor Sue Curran, ministering in Blue Mountain Retreat in Pennsylvania in August 1994; Olen Griff-

ing, at his academy in Dallas, Texas, has documented visions children have had of heaven. Several of them described it in the same way without conferring with each other.

2. Clive Price, "Holy Laughter Hits British Churches," *Charisma,* October 1994, p. 82.

A native of Virginia, Dr. Pickett was raised in North Carolina. Answering the Lord's call to minister the Word of God, she studied at John Wesley College and Virginia Bible College. She has an earned doctorate in the field of theology as well as a doctorate of divinity. She is an ordained minister. She has taught in Bible colleges for more than forty years, and pastored for twenty-seven years.

In 1959, Dr. Pickett became seriously ill with a genetic, life-threatening disease. On April 12, 1959 she was carried into a church service where God miraculously changed the course of her life. She was healed from the disease and baptized in the Holy Spirit. She declares that the greatest thing that ever happened to her occurred when her "Teacher" came in the Person of the Holy Spirit to establish a live-in relationship with her.

Dr. Pickett ministered as a conference evangelist and teacher during the next seven years. In 1966 she moved to Texas where she became affiliated with a large Bible college and served as head of its Bible department as academic dean and, subsequently, as director of the College.

Dr. Pickett and her husband, Leroy, founded Fountain Gate Ministries in 1971. This ministry included an interdominational church, pre-school, academy and college as well as a nationwide tape lending library, video extension program, daily radio program and weekly television ministry.

Since 1988 Dr. Pickett has traveled extensively and is in great demand as a conference speaker and gifted teacher, preparing and encouraging leaders to bring the Church into her inheritance. She and her husband are based at Shekinah Ministries in Blountville, Tennessee.

God's Dream

This book takes us into the heart of God, gives us insight into the Father's dream and reveals the sense of purpose that has motivated everything He has done, is doing and will do before time ceases to be. You will find the answers to the innate questions of every human heart. *$7*

For Such a Time as This

The life of Queen Esther bears greater significance for us than simply her reign as an historical queen. To fulfill His purposes on earth, God must have sons and daughters who determine to respond to the piercing question: Who knows whether you have been brought to the kingdom for such a time as this? *$6*

Presenting the Holy Spirit (2 volumes)

Vol. 1

Speaking from personal and ministerial experience, Dr. Pickett describes the unforgettable impact the vibrant Person of the Holy Spirit makes on human lives and destinies. *$11*

Vol. 2

This second volume presents the work of the Holy Spirit in the individual believer and in the Church. Only as we learn to allow the Holy Spirit to occupy His rightful place in our lives and churches will we be enabled to fulfill the purposes of God. *$13.95*

Amos $5
Child Study $10
Esther $10
Holy Anointing Oil $4
Holy Spirit $10
Hosea $5
How to Search the Scriptures $10
Job $5
Leviticus $4
Proverbs and Ecclesiastes $7
Psalms $6
Romans $6
Ruth $5
Scriptural Study of Five Senses $7
Scripture Numerics $5
Song of Solomon $5
The Anointing $5
The Names of God $5
The Good Shepherd $5
What God's Word Says About Hell $5

A catalog listing other available printed materials as well as audiotapes may also be requested. To order, write or call:

Dr. Fuchsia Pickett
394 Glory Road
Blountville, TN 37617
615-323-2242

U.S. residents, please add 15 percent for shipping costs. Outside the U.S., add 25 percent for shipping. Make checks payable to Dr. Fuchsia Pickett.

If you enjoyed *The Next Move of God*, we would like
to recommend the following books:

Passion for Jesus
by Mike Bickle

Mike Bickle shares from his own life what it means
to be consumed with the personality of God. He
challenges the reader to discover the passion and
splendor of God's personality — a discovery that will
help bring personal wholeness and spiritual maturity.

The Jericho Hour
by Dick Eastman

Christians are breaking through the barriers to evangelism. *The Jericho Hour* tells about that harvest and
how an understanding of strategic-level warfare
prayer, followed by united evangelism, is making it
possible.

Fresh Impact
by Mario Murillo

It's time for Christians to make a real impact! Mario
Murillo shows that believers must stop hiding in the
safe confines of the church and boldly take the
power of the Holy Spirit into America's mainstream
culture.

Available at your local Christian bookstore or from:

Creation House
600 Rinehart Road
Lake Mary, FL 32746
1-800-283-8494